To my friend H.G.W. who
has now join[ed] ... of
a great army ...
"pingles." Along with new
freedoms He also gave us
Some loneliness — to turn
into solitude & creativity.
May This little book help
you to see — and savor! —
Those possibilities.

R.C.S.
10·23·78

LONELINESS

UNDERSTANDING AND DEALING WITH IT

Trite — mixed up sort of a
salad — piece of writing

LONELINESS

UNDERSTANDING AND DEALING WITH IT

HARVEY H. POTTHOFF

Abingdon
Nashville

Loneliness: Understanding and Dealing with It

Library of Congress Cataloging in Publication Data

Potthoff, Harvey H
  Loneliness: understanding and dealing with it.

  1. Loneliness. I. Title.
BF575.L7P67   158'.2   76-13900

ISBN 0-687-22579-5

Text on pages 9 and 58 is from "At a Window" and "Fish Crier" by Carl Sandburg, from *The Complete Poems of Carl Sandburg*. Reprinted by permission of Harcourt Brace Jovanovich, Inc., Publishers.

Text on pages 17 and 31 is from *The Poetry of Robert Frost* edited by Edward Connery Lathem. Copyright 1934, © 1969 by Holt, Rinehart and Winston. Copyright 1936, © 1962 by Robert Frost. Copyright © 1964 by Lesley Frost Ballantine. Reprinted by permission of Holt, Rinehart and Winston, Publishers.

Text on page 31 is from *Identity: Youth and Crisis* by Erik H. Erikson (New York: W. W. Norton & Co., 1968), pp. 140, 141, 233.

Text on page 77 is from "A Loneliness I Never Expected," by Ralph Cokain, © 1972 by The New York Times Company. Reprinted by permission.

Text on page 107 is from *The Life of the Soul* by Samuel H. Miller (New York: Harper & Brothers, 1951), pp. 21-23.

Text on page 121 is from "The Spring and the Fall," by Edna St. Vincent Millay, from *Collected Poems*, Harper & Row. Copyright, 1923, 1951 by Edna St. Vincent Millay and Norma Millay Ellis. Reprinted by permission.

MANUFACTURED BY THE PARTHENON PRESS AT NASHVILLE, TENNESSEE, UNITED STATES OF AMERICA

TO

James Galvin, M.D.

and

Ruth M. Underhill, Ph.D.

How can anyone be so fortunate
as to have friends like these?

Contents

PART THREE
RESOURCES AND STRATEGIES
FOR DEALING WITH LONELINESS

Part One

LONELINESS:
THE DEEPEST PAIN OF ALL

Give me a hunger,
O you gods who sit and give
The world its orders.
Give me hunger, pain and want . . . .

But leave me a little love,
A voice to speak to me in the day end,
A hand to touch me in the dark room
Breaking the long loneliness.

Sandburg

1. To Be Human Is to Experience Loneliness

To be human is to experience the pain of loneliness.

Deep within each of us is the hunger for contact, acceptance, belonging, intimate exchange, responsiveness, support, love, and the touch of tenderness. We experience loneliness because these hungers are not always fed, and because we are sometimes separated from persons and places and things important to us.

Human beings come alive through relationships. Our greatest joys and deepest meanings are experienced through relationships. Meaningful rapport leads to a sense of fulfillment. The lack or loss of such relationships leads to the pain of loneliness.

Loneliness is the feeling of not being meaningfully related. It involves the deep hurt of isolation and separation.

There is something unique or different about each person's experience of loneliness. No two persons travel precisely the same road. Our experiences are uniquely our own. Thus, our isolation is deepened by the awareness that we cannot fully share it with someone else. Loneliness is a deeply private matter. Because relationships are so important to us, loneliness is the deepest pain of all.

Yet, the fact remains that to be human is to experience loneliness. We experience varying forms and degrees of loneliness. All around us are lonely people. Some measure of loneliness seems to be a part of the price of being human. Thus, no one is completely alone in his loneliness. It is important that we learn more about what we are experiencing in the depths of our being when we experience loneliness.

A Personal Word to the Reader

The purpose of this book is simple and practical. It is designed to help the reader better understand his or her own experience of loneliness. It is intended to show that while we cannot escape some experience of loneliness we need not be completely victimized by it. What loneliness does *to* us and *in* us is partly a matter of our own decisions. This book is further designed to present practical suggestions for dealing with loneliness, and to point out available resources.

Human life is inherently hard. Struggle, pain, frustration, and loneliness are part of it. Someone once said, "Be kind to every person you meet; he is having a hard time." The author of the book of Job wrote, "Man is born to trouble as the sparks fly upward" (Job 5:7). This book is not intended to deny the pain which is involved in being truly human, nor does it claim to point the way to a completely serene and peaceful existence. Rather, it is designed to show that the purpose of human existence is meaning in living—and the experience of loneliness can actually contribute to a meaningful life.

The reader is invited to bring his or her own experience of loneliness to the reading of this book. The fact that a person feels lonely does not mean that he is "odd" or "different" or "inadequate" in the business of living. It means that he is hurting, perhaps very deeply. This book is written in the hope that it may help readers move from their present experience of loneliness into a new chapter of life enriched with greater meaning.

Loneliness and Solitude

The experiences of loneliness and solitude differ, even though they are related. It is possible to experience solitude without suffering loneliness. It is important to distinguish between solitude and loneliness.

I had a sister who suffered from multiple sclerosis for many years. Bedridden, she experienced many hours of solitude; yet she possessed a rich inner life. She was related to many persons and events through bonds of thought and feeling and concern. One day she said, "I have more things to do and plan for than I have time." Even in solitude she was not wholly victimized by loneliness.

The Random House Dictionary defines *solitude* as "the state of being or living alone." Solitude suggests being with oneself, without other persons being physically present. The same dictionary defines *lonely* as "destitute of sympathetic or friendly companionship or relationships." It goes on to speak of "a depressing feeling of being alone." Loneliness has to do with internal as well as external conditions. It involves the feeling of not being meaningfully related. It is possible to be lonely in a crowd. But the fact that one is experiencing solitude does not necessarily mean that one is lonely.

Solitude can be renewing and creative. Wordsworth wrote:

> When from our better selves we have too long
> Been parted by the hurrying world, and droop,
> Sick of its business, of its pleasures tired,
> How gracious, how benign, is Solitude.

Sometimes we choose to be alone in order to find ourselves and to get things put together. Most of us need times of solitude. With John Milton we understand that

> Solitude sometimes is best society,
> And short retirement urges sweet return.

Loneliness, on the other hand, involves discomfort and actual pain. It may entail deep distress of spirit. At the heart of the experience of loneliness is the sense of isolation and separation. It may include the sense of being left out, of being rejected, of being estranged, of not being understood, of being abandoned. Loneliness involves the feeling that there is no one and no thing responsive to our deep hunger for support and caring. We are really alone. One of the most painful of all forms of loneliness is that which attends our separation from those who in the past have helped us to forget our aloneness.

Perhaps no one ever completely solves the problem of loneliness. We must all live with some loneliness. Much can be done, however, by way of weaving the pain of loneliness into a pattern of meaningful and productive living. This process involves the creative use of solitude.

The Two Sides of Loneliness

If we are to deal with the experience of loneliness in a constructive way we need to deepen our understanding of it. We need to comprehend what is involved if we are to cope with it creatively.

Throughout this book we shall be probing for a deeper understanding of the dynamics of loneliness. As a start in that direction it is important to recognize that some loneliness is determined by external conditions and some loneliness is determined by factors in ourselves. In most experiences of loneliness, however, both external and internal factors are at work.

Much loneliness can be traced directly to the conditions under which we live. We may be isolated, with a minimum of opportunity to be with people, to talk, laugh, and share with them. We may find ourselves in situations where the people about us have different interests from our own. Sometimes we are with people who do not share our values and concerns, who speak a different language. As one grows older he may feel left out of things, as though he had outlived his own generation. Sometimes we are forced into situations involving isolation—in work and unemployment, in sickness, in family. Isolation and loneliness are closely related.

Much of the meaning and joy of life comes through relationships with *persons* and *places* and *things*. Sometimes our life situation changes so that we are removed from the persons, places, and things which have emotional meaning for us. We feel lonely and out of touch.

Recently I was talking with a student from a foreign country. He was terribly lonely in the midst of people who spoke a language which was not his own, who ate food different from that to which he was accustomed, who laughed at jokes he could not understand, who had customs which seemed strange to him. He felt left out. He was homesick and lonely—yearning for persons and places and things which were a part of his inner life.

So it often is with persons who move from some familiar setting into a place where things are different. In our time there is much moving about. There is much uprootedness. We feel separated from the persons, places, and things which have nurtured us and made us truly alive. Feeling cut off, we are often victims of the pain of loneliness. Just as a person can be "worried sick," so he can become "lonely sick." And when we are "lonely sick" our whole being experiences distress. Body, mind, and spirit are involved.

There is a second side to the experience of loneliness. As we have seen, some loneliness can be traced to external circumstances. But some loneliness can be traced to our own difficulties in relating, in adjusting, in communicating, in sharing. We feel locked up within ourselves. Persons vary greatly in the ease with which they can reach out to others in communication.

Persons who find it relatively easy to talk to others, who experience little difficulty in meeting new people, and who enjoy group experiences, cannot fully comprehend how different it is with some other human beings. Many persons desperately wish that they could be more open and more communicative, but they find it extremely difficult. They are lonely.

Sometimes we try to cover up our timidity and difficulty in communicating. We conceal our deeper feelings and desire for true communication. Robert Frost spoke of this human tendency in one of his poems:

We make ourselves a place apart
  Behind light words that tease and flout,
But oh, the agitated heart
  Till someone really find us out.

But so with all, from babes that play
  At hide-and-seek to God afar,
So all who hide too well away
  Must speak and tell us where they are.[1]

To enter into the life about us, to speak and tell where we are, is not easy for many persons. Sometimes it is easier to withdraw, to be silent, and to build walls of separation between ourselves and others. There are many reasons why we follow this lonely route. Sometimes we are the victims of unfortunate conditions and relationships in infancy and childhood. Sometimes we have experienced rejection or failure in human relations. The result may be that we are afraid to take the risks involved in reaching out, in relating, and in caring. There are times when an understanding friend or counselor may help us deal with such inner blocks to communication.

Sometimes our attitudes create barriers to meaningful relationships. We may keep waiting for the world to come to us, forgetting that sometimes we need to extend the encouraging word, the friendly touch, the open and grateful spirit. Sometimes we prefer the painful path of loneliness to the effort involved in reaching out to someone else's loneliness.

We often sell short our own capacity to participate in the life around us. Our fears and timidities may hold us back from taking in some of the goodness, beauty, and friendliness which is close at hand.

There are times when we misjudge other persons and assume that they are cold or indifferent. So we turn from them, forgetting that people sometimes wear masks of coldness and indifference to hide their loneliness.

If we are serious about coming to terms with the problem of loneliness we need to be willing to acknowledge that we are lonely. We must try to understand some of the reasons why we feel the pain of lonelinesss. Upon examination we shall find that some loneliness can be traced to external circumstances, some of which may be beyond our control, and some of which can be changed. On the other hand, some loneliness may be traced to blockages and attitudes within ourselves.

No human being lives under ideal circumstances. Life is offered to us on quite different terms. Life was offered to Helen Keller on different terms from those offered to Albert Schweitzer. Yet, each accepted the gift of life and made something significant out of it.

It is the lot of some persons to experience more of loneliness than others. We all have limitations and handicaps; but we also have certain capacities and strengths, even though they may seem minimal. Although our external circumstances may appear to be extremely limiting, there is an inner world which can tip the scales between despair and hope—between being victimized by loneliness and reaching out to be in touch with other persons and things. Except in relatively rare cases, we can take some step or steps toward the alleviation of loneliness. We may even take steps toward finding meaning and deeper self-awareness through our experience.

I know a woman, now in her sixties, who has travelled a difficult road in her lifetime. She has outlived many things. Fortunately, she has managed to maintain an interest in things and people. She has kept a sense of humor. She has also managed to keep alive the spark of hope. A few days ago she said, "I have known much loneliness in my life. But looking back over the years, I see that it has not been without its meaning. I know myself better, I think I am more sensitive to others, I have made discoveries about life—through loneliness."

The Contemporary Experience of Loneliness

The experience of loneliness is as old as the human race. In every age persons have had to cope with this agonizing problem. Nevertheless, it is probably accurate to say that loneliness is an increasingly pervasive fact in the modern world. This may seem strange since there are more people in the world than ever before. Persons come together in larger and larger cities. Modern methods of communication make it possible for persons to talk with each other in a matter of moments throughout the world. American and Russian astronauts cooperate in space ventures. How can it be that the experience of loneliness is increasing? Having access to so many *things,* how can we feel so much emptiness of spirit?

Yet, this seems to be the case. Numberless books and articles have been written in recent years dealing with the themes of alienation, estrangement, and the search for meaning. Artists, philosophers, psychologists, theologians, and dramatists have spoken in varied languages of the contemporary sense of fragmentation, detachment, and isolation. Erich Fromm has summarized a point of view held by many perceptive observers: "The deepest need of man, then, is the need to overcome his separateness, to leave the prison of his aloneness .... Modern man is alienated from himself, from his fellow men, and from nature. He has been transformed into a commodity, experiences his life forces as an investment which must bring him the maximum profit obtainable under existing market conditions .... While everybody tries to be as close as possible to the rest, everybody remains utterly alone, pervaded by the deep sense of insecurity, anxiety and guilt which always results when human separateness cannot be overcome ... man overcomes his conscious despair by the routine of amusement, the passive consumption of sounds and sights offered by the amusement industry; furthermore by the satisfaction of buying ever new things, and soon exchanging them for others."[2]

In reflecting on the changes which are taking place in our world I sometimes recall the small town in southern Minnesota where I lived for some years as a boy. The village bell tolled whenever anyone in town died. In this symbolic way it was said that the life and death of every human being was important to the entire community.

Now living in a large city I see many funeral processions. Sometimes I do not even wonder who has died. But occasionally I recall the tolling of the bell in that small town I knew as a boy, and I realize how the conditions of our lives change—and how we, in turn, are changed in the process. It is difficult to maintain a real sense of community in the modern world, and without this our feeling of detachment increases.

To understand our own experience of loneliness and better understand the pervasive loneliness of our times, we need to recognize the influences which act upon us. There are many factors which encourage a sense of isolation and rob us of a sense of identity and worth as individuals.

We experience rapid change—some of which undercuts familiar sources of security.

We move more frequently than in past generations—with the attendant problems of uprootedness.

We experience "bigness"—in government, in business, in labor, in education, in the universe—and in the process we lose the sense of importance in ourselves and in our decision-making. We want to be participants, but at many points we feel left out. Society too often seems to say "You are not needed," and this is the most devastating message we can receive.

We experience the development of technology with its many benefits, but we also encounter the threat of dehumanization. Erich Fromm has written: "A specter is stalking in our midst whom only a few see with clarity. . . . It is a new spectre: A completely mechanized society, devoted to maximum material output and consumption, directed by computers; and in this social process, man himself is being transformed into a part of the total machine."[3] On television we witness the drama of life and death around the world, but often feel no sense of personal involvement.

We experience changing relationships in the family. An increasing number of persons do not share in the experiences and relationships of support and meaning traditionally associated with many families.

With the rapid expansion of urban centers many persons experience numerous *contacts* while experiencing a minimum of meaningful *relationships*. Martin Buber wrote that "All real living is meeting." We attend many meetings in which no one really meets.

We are subject to endless attempts to sell us something. Public relations techniques are used to project images of ourselves, of various products, and of the good life which may or may not have validity.

Increasingly we buy things that are ready-made. We attend athletic contests in which professional athletes perform for us. In the process we may lose touch with the products of our own labor and we lose the sense of identity and fulfillment which come from involvement in the creation of that by which we live. There is a loneliness which attends the image of ourselves as basically spectators and consumers. Sustaining and enriching relationships call for participation.

Astounding achievements have been made in the field of medical science. As a result, more persons live to advanced years, multiplying the loneliness which often attends old age. In the light of medical advances, human beings are now called upon to make difficult decisions pertaining to life and death control. There can be agonizing loneliness in making judgments which affect the life and death of those we love the most. Responsible involvement in the modern world sometimes comes at the cost of loneliness.

In *Paths of Loneliness* Margaret Wood asked, "What is there in us, or in the society of our time, that makes each of us a solitary individual, separate and apart, alone, yet needing others and needed by them?" If our analysis has truth in it, many factors contribute to the pervasive loneliness of our time. Indeed, there is much loneliness which goes unrecognized as such. Health of mind and spirit requires that we seek fuller understanding of these important matters. We need both insight and personal strategies for dealing with loneliness in ways which lead toward a more meaningful quality of life. No one of us can escape the pain of loneliness, but loneliness need not be the final truth of our existence.

The Ultimate Loneliness

Thus far in our discussion we have distinguished aloneness, solitude, and loneliness.

A part of the greatness of the human creature is his aloneness. There is something unique about each person. Because we have a center which is our own we can affirm our own identity, we can observe the world, we can exercise a measure of freedom, we can make decisions. Aloneness is a precondition of love. Love recognizes the worth and uniqueness of the other; it seeks the real center.

Because of our aloneness we need the experience of solitude. As we have seen, solitude can be creative and renewing. We need time alone when we can collect our thoughts, reflect on who and where we are, and draw on deep resources of spirit. Solitude can reveal the glory of being alone. It is required in the deepest of relationships.

Loneliness is the feeling of not being meaningfully related. Aloneness and solitude may issue in loneliness, but not necessarily so. One of the central questions in our existence is "In your aloneness and in your solitude, to what or to whom are you related?" If our answer is "no one" or "no thing," then we are truly lonely.

The great religions of the world raise the question of our most ultimate relationship or relationships. In varied ways they affirm the reality of a source, a wisdom, an order, a providence, a grace, or a destiny to which we are related in life and death. Great religion affirms, "You are not alone." Thus, great religion alleviates the pain of loneliness and brings meaning into existence. It affirms aloneness and solitude and an ultimate relatedness all at the same time.

One of the most insightful analyses of religious experience is found in Alfred North Whitehead's book *Religion in the Making.* Whitehead wrote:

Religion is what the individual does with his own solitariness. It runs through three stages, if it evolves to its final satisfaction. It is the transition from God the void to God the enemy, and from God the enemy to God the companion. Thus religion is solitariness; and if you are never solitary, you are never religious . . . .

The great religious conceptions which haunt the imaginations of civilized mankind are scenes of solitariness: Prometheus chained to his rock, Mahomet brooding in the desert, the meditations of the Buddha, the solitary Man on the Cross. It belongs to the depth of the religious spirit to have felt forsaken, even by God . . . .

In its solitariness the spirit asks, What, in the way of value, is the attainment of life? And it can find no such value till it has merged its individual claim with that of the objective universe. Religion is world-loyalty.[4]

As Whitehead so vividly suggests, we come to a crisis point in our existence when we are confronted by the fact of our aloneness and our uniqueness. In a deep sense it is true that by nature we are separated; we are who and what we are, and not someone or something else. To exist as an individual is to stand out, and thus, to be apart. What, then, happens in the depths of our being when it comes to us with full force that we are alone? Our first reaction may be that what we are up against is a vast *void*—nothing. We may come to the place where we are convinced that what we are up against and subject to in life and death is an enemy over against us. But having lived through these stages the religious spirit comes to affirm a cosmic affiliation, a responsiveness which judges and sustains, a Real-Other conferring sanctity on our existence—God the companion. In his aloneness and solitude the person of religious faith feels, "I am not alone."

In this faith the psalmist said, "My flesh and my heart may fail, but God is the strength of my heart and my portion for ever" (Psalm 73:26). "Even though I walk through the valley of the shadow of death, I fear no evil; for thou art with me; thy rod and thy staff, they comfort me" (Psalm 23:4). In this faith the imprisoned Dietrich Bonhoeffer, facing execution, wrote of his intermingled doubt and belief, love and hate, trust and fear, and then concluded saying:

> Who am I? They mock me, these lonely
> questions of mine.
> Whoever I am, Thou knowest, O God, I am
> thine!

It is the mark of the religious spirit to affirm the companionship of God in life and death, in the high and low tides of the spirit. If in the extremities of

25

life one cries out "My God, my God, why hast thou forsaken me?" (Psalm 22:1), the cry is still addressed to God who in some sense is believed to be there. The word *religion* in a root sense means "to bind"—thus, religion is the affirmation of an ultimate relatedness, an ultimate belonging. Gordon Allport has written: "A man's religion is the audacious bid he makes to bind himself to creation and to the Creator. It is his ultimate attempt to enlarge and complete his own personality by finding the supreme context in which he rightly belongs."[5]

The ultimate loneliness is the pain of feeling that there is no depth which speaks to our depth, there is no integrity which upholds us in our integrity, there is no responsiveness in relation to our deepest needs and highest aspirations. In our aloneness there is only void.

As we shall be seeing, there are resources for dealing with loneliness. Some of these have to do with persons, places, and things as well as our own attitudes. But beyond all these there is religious faith. To affirm belief in God is to affirm the good news that in life and death we are related to a Real-Other worthy of our trust and devotion.

John Gardner has written:

He [man] has throughout history shown a compelling need to arrive at conceptions of the universe *in terms of which he could count his own life as meaningful.* He wants to know where *he* fits into the scheme of things. He wants to understand how the great facts of the objective world relate to *him* and what they imply for his behavior. He wants to know what significance may be found in his own existence, the succeeding generations of his kind and the vivid events of his inner life. He seeks some kind of meaningful framework in which to understand (or at least reconcile himself to) the indignities of chance and circumstance and the fact of death. A number of philosophers and scientists have told him sternly that he must not expect answers to that sort of question, but he pays little heed. He wants, in the words of Kierkegaard, "a truth which is true for me." He seeks conceptions of the universe that give dignity, purpose and sense to his own existence.[6]

There is a loneliness which springs from the feeling that one lives out his days in an alien universe. There is an ultimate loneliness rooted in the feeling that one is really not cared about in a final sense. Religion persists in the life of the human race because it speaks to that loneliness.

Can Any Good Come Out of Our Loneliness?

Is loneliness something simply to be endured? Or can something of meaning come out of it? Some years ago Clark Moustakas wrote a little book entitled *Loneliness*. He described the basic message of his book as being "that loneliness is a condition of human life, an experience of being human which enables the individual to sustain, extend, and deepen his humanity." Obviously he believed that some good can come out of loneliness, if we will have it so.

Apparently what he said was confirmed in the experience of many persons. He later wrote a book entitled *The Touch of Loneliness* in which he published messages received from many readers. They tell how through their experiences of loneliness they learned important things about themselves, became more aware of the needs of others, discovered deep resources of spirit they had not known existed, and grew in awareness and sensitivity.

Nothing can be said or written which entirely

removes the reality or pain of loneliness. But it is good to know that the pain need not all be wasted. Out of the deepest hurts there sometimes comes some harvest of the spirit—if we wish it so to be.

In his book *Man's Search for Meaning* Dr. Viktor Frankl reports the reactions of persons to the indignities endured in Nazi prison camps. These are his words:

A human being is not one thing among others; *things* determine each other, but *man* is ultimately self-determining. What he becomes—within the limits of endowment and environment—he has made out of himself. In the concentration camps, for example, in this living laboratory and on this testing ground, we watched and witnessed some of our comrades behave like swine while others behaved like saints. Man has both potentialities within himself; which one is actualized depends on decisions but not on conditions . . . .

What was really needed was a fundamental change in our attitude toward life. We had to learn ourselves and, furthermore, we had to teach the despairing men, that it did not really matter what we expected from life, but rather what life expected from us. . . . Life ultimately means taking the responsibility to find the right answer to its problems and to fulfill the tasks which it constantly sets for each individual.[7]

Our attitudes and decisions *do* make a difference when we are imprisoned in loneliness. Here is a part of the greatness of our humanity. To suffer greatly, and in the midst of our suffering to be open to what loneliness can bring, is a road to life's deeper meaning.

When we are in the midst of the experience of loneliness our first wish is that it would go away. The causes of some loneliness can, indeed, be changed, corrected, or removed; but there are other forms of loneliness which must be endured. We cannot change the fact of the death of a loved one, of a devastating change in our situation, of a mistake which cannot be undone. The question then emerges: "Can any good come out of my loneliness?" "Can I hope for anything more than the power to endure what must be endured?"

There is hope for the person who can admit his loneliness, who is free to express the pain of it, and who then acknowledges that there may be some first steps he can take in dealing with it. In the next section of our study we shall consider some specific experiences and dimensions of loneliness. We shall consider available resources and some of the things we can do in affirming that we need not be completely victimized by the external conditions of our lives.

Part Two

THE VARIED TIMES AND FORMS OF LONELINESS

They cannot scare me with their empty spaces
Between stars—on stars where no human race is.
I have it in me so much nearer home
To scare myself with my own desert places.

Frost

A civilization can be measured by the meaning which it gives to the full life cycle, for such meaning, or lack of it, cannot fail to reach into the beginnings of the next generation, and thus into the chances of others to meet ultimate questons with some clarity and strength . . . .

If . . . man can make himself sick and survive in a fashion that no other creature would call living, he also has the capacity for diagnosis and cure, critique and change. These in turn rely on a revitalization of strength, a revival of values, a restoration of productive forces. It is in this sense that I claim for the life cycle a generational principle which would tend to perpetuate a series of vital virtues from *hope* in infancy to *wisdom* in old age.

Erikson

2. Loneliness and the Life Cycle

The book of Ecclesiastes tells us

> For everything there is a season, and a time
> for every matter under heaven:
> a time to be born, and a time to die;
> a time to plant, and a time to pluck up
> what is planted.

(Ecclesiastes 3:1-2)

In the spirit of that ancient statement we might add: For everything there is a season: a time to be born, a time to be an infant, a time to be a child, a time to be an adolescent, a time to be a young adult, a time to be middle-aged, a time to experience the later years, and a time to die. Each of these times has its important place in the total human career. Distinctive meanings attend each period. If life is to unfold and be fulfilled in the most wholesome way, certain things need to be achieved in the experiencing of each time. The glory of a life well lived is the glory of moving from time to time, from chapter to chapter, from strength to strength, reaping those qualities of personhood each time affords.

Each chapter of life involves us in certain forms of loneliness. What happens to us and in us through that loneliness is a matter of the greatest importance. To be a stranger to the seasons of life, to deny or resist the normal movement of life, is to experience tragic loneliness. But to be open to the potential meanings of each step along the way and to be open to the resources which help us deal with the forms of loneliness more or less peculiar to each chapter, is to experience growth, fulfillment, and wholeness of being.

In this chapter we shall explore a fascinating truth: each time of life involves us in certain forms of separation at the same time that it opens the door to the possibility of new forms of relationships. The separations may be extremely painful (involving loneliness); but these same separations may lead to fulfilling relationships. The person who has learned to live in harmony with the unfolding character of life has achieved the artistry of living—affirming the natural separations and relationships which life involves.

Loneliness in Infancy

Perhaps it sounds strange to speak of loneliness in infancy. How can an infant be lonely? But some of the most important roots of loneliness are to be found in infancy, and what happens to a human being as he experiences loneliness during this period may profoundly affect his later life.

To be born is to experience separation. In being expelled from the womb the infant leaves a world where every need was supplied and enters a world where supply is not always equal to demand. Along with the hunger for food is the hunger for contact, tenderness, and intimate interaction. In the separation from one's mother is an experience related to the origins of loneliness. Not all needs are met.

Child psychiatrist René Spitz has written of the crucial importance of the mother-infant "dialogue," involving reciprocity, the interchange of action and response. The sense of the animate, and the capacity for development are rooted in this

He may also move toward the most important fruits of childhood: satisfaction in the sense of being a person; growing competence in relation to bodily functions and the use of language; initiative related to participation in play and other activities; acceptance on the part of significant persons; intimate exchange with chums, friends, and loved ones; and an emerging conscience.

Childhood is a time of discovery, of wonder, of mystery and frustration. The discovery includes the emerging awareness of masculine and feminine roles, an emerging awareness of how parents relate to each other, and the encounter with persons and things outside the family. Wonder and mystery attend natural processes. Frustration accompanies the awareness of tension between parents, the loss of a parent, unmet needs and unfulfilled desires, and the many, many unanswered questions.

Childhood, like all other times of life, involves separation—one is no longer an infant, one's relationship to his mother is changed, one experiences growing pains. But if there are separations in childhood there is also the possibility of new and rewarding relationships. Childhood, then, is not carefree. Like all other times of life it is a mixture of frustrations and possibilities, of disappointments and enjoyments. How much we need understanding adults who know something of the pains and joys and questions in the heart of a child!

Children have much to teach adults. Many years ago it was said, "A little child shall lead them." There would be much less loneliness in the world if adults were willing to learn from children and enter their world through shared play and conversation. Transgenerational communication is one of the most important roads to the alleviation of loneliness and the experience of joy through relationships.

What are some of the most vivid memories associated with your childhood? Perhaps in recalling these we are better prepared to share the experience of children around us. For children, like adults, live in the tension of separation. It is out of that tension that both loneliness and growth come into being.

A few days ago I spent the afternoon with my friends Karen, aged nine, Robert, aged seven, and Paul, aged three. We played with a frisbee, we went to the zoo, we rode a miniature train, and then we just sat and talked. In our being together I was reminded again that if there is a generation gap, there is also a bond between generations, for all of us experience separation in our own way. And if there is loneliness, there is also love.

The Loneliness of Adolescence

In the years of adolescence the young person experiences awesome and bewildering changes in physiology, physiognomy, and outlook. He experiences the need and the will to be weaned away from his parents at the same time that he feels a linkage with them.

He experiences extraordinarily difficult conflicts involving impulsiveness and restraints, a sense of loyalty in the midst of diverse value systems, and a sense of the ideal conflicting with his perception of what actually is. No longer a child and not yet an adult in an adult world, the adolescent agonizes over his own identity. Involved in a variety of roles, some of which are conflicting, he wonders who he really is. Painfully he seeks identity in relation to

37

the opposite sex, to family history, and to causes of various kinds. Someone has referred to "the turbulent sea of adolescence." It is, indeed, a time of storm and stress. It is also a time involving loneliness.

Theodore Lidz has written:

> It is a time of physical and emotional metamorphosis during which the youth feels estranged from the self the child had known. It is a time of seeking: a seeking inward to find who one is; a searching outward to locate one's place in life; a longing for another with whom to satisfy cravings for intimacy and fulfillment. It is a time of turbulent awakening to love and beauty but also of days darkened by loneliness and despair. It is a time of carefree wandering of the spirit through realms of fantasy and in pursuit of idealistic visions, but also of disillusionment and disgust with the world and with the self. It can be a time of adventure with wonderful episodes of reckless folly but also of shame and regret that linger. The adolescent lives with a vibrant sensitivity that carries to ecstatic heights and lowers to almost untenable depths.[3]

Because this is a time in which the adolescent feels separated from what has been at the same time that he seeks new relationships and a new identity, it is a time of tremendous possibility. But because the adolescent is not sure who and what and where he is, it is a time involving deep loneliness.

Erik Erikson has written of the great importance of "confirming adults and affirming peers" to adolescent youth. He points to the fact that "cultures, societies, religions offer the adolescent the nourishment of some truth in rites and rituals of confirmation as a member of a totem, a clan or a faith, a nation or a class, which henceforth is to be his super-family." In the loneliness of adolescence there is great need for the understanding, support- ing, and affirming relationship of persons and groups. In the confusions of this period there are the ambivalent desires to revolt and to conform. And in the midst of that ambivalence, there is loneliness.

The wonder of life's unfolding is no more dramatically revealed than during this time, for what one carries out of the struggles of these years profoundly influences the direction of life ahead. Painful as the loneliness of adolescence is, it has potential for meaning. And if adolescence brings loneliness, it also brings excitement, joy, and expectation.

Loneliness in Young Adulthood

"The glory of God is man fully alive," said one of the founders of the early church.

The purpose of life is to live and fulfill the human role. The purpose of being a human being is to become more fully human through the chapters of life.

The glory of young adulthood is in the possibilities offered for an unfolding experience of being human as an adult. It is a time for becoming more fully alive.

Young adulthood involves separation from much that belongs to the world of adolescence although it also includes much out of that past experience. New relationships are established during this time which give direction to the rest of life. These relationships carry with them the potential for satisfaction and fulfillment—but also for loneliness.

At the heart of young adulthood is the search for basic identifications around which life can unfold and mature. These identifications are frequently, if not usually, found through choices and decisions which are made during this period: the choice of a partner and the establishment of a family, the choice of a vocation or vocations, decisions relating to life goals, the choice of groups with which one is to identify, decisions involving the setting of priorities and values, decisions relating to involvement or noninvolvement in community life, deci sions pertaining to matters of religious orientation and commitment.

These varied choices and decisions issue in life-styles. Obviously, they have much to do with the sorts of meaning and fulfillment one finds in life.

A few days ago an active young adult said to me, "I don't think the book you are writing is for me—I am never lonely." It is hard to believe that any young adult is *never* lonely. But it is true that most young adults have opportunities for meeting people. And since the young adult is at the peak of his physical and mental vigor he can more readily become involved than in some other periods of life.

Loneliness varies from person to person in early adulthood. When it goes deep and poses a truly major problem (and my own belief is that this is often the case), it can most often be traced to disappointments, failures, and frustrations in establishing some of the basic identifications of which we have spoken.

To experience serious disappointment and frustration in the marriage relationship (with loss of real communication), to be deprived of the joys of a good marriage, to be unhappy in one's work and to feel separated from the fruits of one's own labor, to feel out of touch with groups that support and enrich, to lack goals which give a sense of direction to life, to be lacking a philosophy which helps tie things together, is to experience a loss of basic identifications which may well issue in deep unhappiness and loneliness.

In contemporary America we see the loneliness which often accompanies the role of the single young adult or the single parent and the loneliness which accompanies being cast in working conditions for which one has little enthusiasm. As we have seen, some loneliness is related to factors in ourselves; but many young adults experience forms of loneliness which can be traced to imbalances and unresolved problems in our society.

In his play *Death of a Salesman* Arthur Miller portrays Biff saying, "I just can't take hold, Mom, I can't take hold of some kind of life." Young adulthood is a time for taking hold of some kind of life through significant identifications. To fail or to be frustrated in that is to experience separation and loneliness.

By the same token, young adulthood is a time for nurturing relationships and interests which will bear fruit throughout the years of life. The strategies for dealing with loneliness which the young adult adopts are of great importance; they will influence his life-style for years to come. To recognize the inevitability of some deep loneliness, and then realize that such loneliness can actually be creative, is one of the most important achievements of young adulthood.

Loneliness in the Middle Years

Recently two couples in their middle years were in a small group. The difference in outlook was striking. One couple was obviously excited about the things they were doing and the plans they were making; they had hopes and expectations to talk about. They were *interested* and *interesting*. The other couple had a very different outlook. They seemed to feel that their real life was over, now that the children were grown and gone. Life seemed to be at best a dull routine, with nothing in particular to live for or look forward to. They were lonely.

How can it be that two couples—whose external circumstances are in many ways similar—can have such different outlooks on life and feelings about life? In seeking answers for that question we confront again the issue of meaning in living. Loneliness is the feeling of not being meaningfully related—to other persons, to work and play, to interests and causes, to the seasons of life.

The middle years, like other times of life, involve both separations and possibilities for meaningful new relationships. In these years life is likely to flatten out or flower out. Which direction life takes depends in part on external circumstances and in part on personal decisions.

The middle years are likely to bring changes and separations. The children are no longer children; they may have established homes of their own. In the middle years one discovers that some dreams long held are realized, but others will never be. There is often a gap between what one *wished* to become and what one *has* become. One must live with limited realizations. In the middle years one realizes he cannot remake his past; the record thus far is written. The question is how to relate to one's past and go on from there. What meanings one proposes to seek in the remainder of life becomes a paramount question.

The middle years also can bring deep satisfactions—in children and grandchildren, in the sense of significant accomplishments and relationships, in the freedom from many worries.

The middle years offer significant opportunities for deepening the sense of being meaningfully related to life. To be sure, one may think he or she is too busy for such things; but the fact remains that the kinds of growth experienced and relationships nurtured in the middle years makes a crucial difference in the rest of life. There is much loneliness in the world which can be traced to a failure to live the middle years in ways which are spiritually fulfilling.

Dr. Richard Cabot wrote that there are four things by which we truly live: work, play, love, and worship. In the middle years our inner lives need to be nourished by all four. I should like to add the experience of beauty. The poet insisted that "beauty is its own excuse for being." In the middle years we need to grow in those strengths and appreciations related to the inner life. We need to take time to be renewed through the world of nature, through play, through friendship and love, through worship, through beauty in art and music and the world about us. In the middle years we need to find "margins in our living"—and we need a sense of humor. Lacking these things, the strains and stresses of life will keep mounting and life will seem more like a rat race than an adventure, more like a burden than a gift. Lacking renewal of the inner life deep loneliness is likely to set in during the middle years. One can have much—and still feel empty.

The middle years offer the opportunity to move

toward a mature view of life, the universe, and self. In the perspective of the years we need a philosophy or faith which helps to tie things together making some sense of the drama of life. One of the temptations of the middle years is to block out matters of ultimate concern. One may choose inwardly to deny that he is growing older, endeavoring to play the role of the young adult. One may give himself or herself with increased fervor to more and more activities. One can bury himself in things. But this life-style has in it the seeds of loneliness, for this cannot go on forever. We become more fully and deeply human not only in doing, but in *being* and *appreciating* and *creating* and *caring* and *relating*. That is why the setting of priorities and the endeavor to "see life whole" is important in the middle years. The middle years see the fulfillment of much that has gone before; but this is also a time of preparation for what lies ahead. It is good news, that for most of us life need not wear out or flatten out in the middle years—it can flower out. And in flowering out there are resources for dealing with loneliness and other threats to the sense of well-being.

Loneliness in the Later Years

Persons in our culture who reach sixty-five have a life expectancy of over twelve years. Persons who reach the age of eighty have an expectation of another ten years. Whether the later years begin somewhere in the fifties or somewhere in the sixties is perhaps a debatable point, but it is not important for our present discussion. The main point is that there is a great deal of living to be done in the later years.

If great loneliness is often experienced in the later years, so is deep meaning. Among the blessings of the later years are the enjoyment of the fruits of a lifetime, the freedom from nagging pressures, the time to do things long postponed, the opportunities to develop new interests, and the sense of well-being in relation to things accomplished and things to look forward to—at least for some.

The later years, like all other chapters of life, involve separations and possibilities for new relationships of meaning.

The later years may bring retirement and separation from the work in which one has long been involved. Persons respond very differently to that experience. There may be separations from friends and loved ones who have had deep emotional meaning for us. It is estimated that 50 percent of women who have been married and reach the later sixties have lost their spouses; 20 percent of the men who were married have lost their wives. Women tend to live longer than men. The loss of a mate and the necessity of being alone in the later years can bring agonizing loneliness.

There are separations involved in changing roles within the community. One may be made to feel that he or she is not needed. As one becomes increasingly dependent on others, there may be the feeling of "being a burden." Problems of reduced income and declining strength may add to the difficulties of the later years. Probably every reader of these pages knows some individual, long active, now increasingly dependent on others, feeling not needed, alone, and lonely. We shall speak of these matters in a later chapter.

It is important to recognize, however, that life in the late fifties, sixties, and beyond represent a significant chapter in the life cycle. It need not be a time for stagnation. We all know persons who reveal a love of life in their later years. I think of my friend who in her ninety-first year announced that from now on she is going to celebrate her birthdays in reverse beginning at eighty-nine. She hopes to make it to fifty! I think of a retired friend—almost blind—who is an avid sports fan and keeps up with games of many kinds around the nation. Sometimes he even sends advice to the coaches. I think of three of the finest teachers I ever had—persons who have profoundly influenced my life—who were all in their later years.

In the later years one is more free to leave some things behind even as one is more free to savor memories and achievements. It is a time for planning each day as though it were a new life in miniature, with someone to call or write to or remember in some way; something to do and read and share; something to anticipate. The later years provide opportunities for reaching out to the loneliness of others. Nothing makes a person so strong as a call for help. Around us are persons to whom we can mean something.

The later years invite us to recall our roots and deepen some of the traditions to which we are related. It is a time to affirm one's own self and one's life story. Erik Erikson reminds us that the finest fruit of the stages of life is that quality of being he calls integrity. He describes it in this way:

> Only he who in some way has taken care of things and people and has adapted himself to the triumphs and disappointments of

being the originator of others and the generator of things and ideas only he may grow the fruit of [life's] stages . . . .

It is the acceptance of one's own and only life cycle and of the people who have become significant to it as something that had to be and that, by necessity, permitted of no substitutions. It thus means a new different love of one's parents, free of the wish that they should have been different, and an acceptance of the fact that one's life is one's own responsibility. It is a sense of comradeship with men and women of distant times and of different pursuits, who have created orders and objects and sayings conveying human dignity and love . . . the possessor of integrity is ready to defend the dignity of his own life style against all physical and economic threats. For he knows that an individual life is the coincidence of but one life cycle with but one segment of history; and that for him all human integrity stands and falls with the one style of integrity of which he partakes.[4]

It is almost certain that loneliness will be experienced in the later years. But what that loneliness comes to mean to us is partly our own decision. There can be dignity and integrity in loneliness. And loneliness loses some of its sting when there are inner companions of the spirit—and when there is faith.

There is a saying to the effect that "what gets your attention gets you." Preoccupation with oneself leads toward a life of withdrawal and loneliness. Attention to events about us, the interests and concerns of others, the companionship of books and music and significant persons we call to mind leads to a quality of aliveness even when physical strength may be declining. An unknown author wrote:

> Age is a quality of mind.
> If you have left your dreams behind,
> If hope is cold
> If you no longer look ahead
> And love of life within your heart is dead—
> Then you are old.

Dr. Olga Knopf, practicing psychiatry at the age of eighty-seven, has given this wise counsel:

There is real satisfaction in old age—if you will take pride in what you still can do. I have acquired judgment about many things I've known all my life but never knew what to do with them. Connections, too, have fallen into place—probably because I never really had time to think about these things before.

You lose time only if you look back and cry. *If you look forward the world is yours!* This is real—it's not put on.[5]

In his later years Dr. Harry Emerson Fosdick illustrated the forward and the outward look which keeps renewing the inner life and which counteracts loneliness. He said:

I am now an old man, and I must add that I am enjoying it . . . at threescore-years-and-eighteen I find this generation the most stimulating, exciting, provocative—yes, promising—era I have ever seen or read about. I want to see what is going to happen next . . . . there are open doors of possibility for good as well as evil, which did not exist when I was born; and though I am an old man, I share at least a little of the hopeful spirit of the young, facing life, as Lowell sang, with "the rays of morn on their white Shields of Expectation!"[6]

Using Loneliness or Being Its Victim

The ancient stoics taught that wisdom in living involves distinguishing what is within our control and what is beyond our control. That wisdom is reflected in this familiar prayer:

O God, help me to change what can and should be changed. Help me to accept with serenity that which cannot be changed. Then, give me the wisdom to know one from the other.

As we live through various chapters of life we quickly discover that there are some things beyond our control. To acknowledge them as part of life and to come to terms with them with some measure of serenity is essential for meaningful living. Every human being lives within limitations of some sort. On the other hand, there are many things that can be changed. Furthermore, our attitude toward what can and cannot be changed makes a crucial difference.

So it is with the experience of loneliness. Some loneliness can be traced to conditions which we can do something about. Some loneliness is related to events and circumstances over which we have little or no external control. But even in the latter case, there are things we can do about our attitudes and responses. In the long run we either use our loneliness or we become victims of it.

In the office of an educator whose specialty is helping people think in terms of what is ahead for them, there is a plaque which reads: "I lived half my life before I realized that it was a do-it-yourself job." In commenting on this Walter Menninger has written, "There's a big difference between the search for identity and the mature recognition that when it comes down to the wire you have to assume responsibility for what you are and what you wish to accomplish in life." Childhood and adolescence involve the search for identity. Young adulthood, the middle years, and the later years hopefully bring the perspective and wisdom of maturity with the awareness that we have it in ourselves to make important decisions about what life is going to mean to us. In a real sense, the wonder of being human lies in the capacity to assume responsibility for our own lives.

In this chapter we have pursued an interesting and important theory: We need to see life "whole" in terms of living through infancy, childhood, adolescence, young adulthood, the middle years, and the later years. Each stage of life involves both separations and possibilities for new relationships and in the tension of separation and possibility is the strong likelihood of loneliness. We are now saying that what the experience of loneliness does *to* us and *in* us is partly a matter of our own attitudes and responses.

It is possible to experience considerable loneliness and still live a meaningful life, provided we have learned to live in harmony with the time processes and found interests beyond ourselves.

The author of the Ninetieth Psalm wrote of the brevity and hardships of human life. He also spoke of the greatness and enduring reality of God. He concluded by offering a prayer:

> So teach us to number our days
>   that we may get a heart of wisdom.
>
> Let thy work be manifest to thy servants,
>   and thy glorious power to their children.
> Let the favor of the Lord our God be upon us,
>   and establish thou the work of our hands upon us,
>   yea, the work of our hands establish thou it.
>   (Psalm 90:12, 16-17)

The author of those words knew the experience of loneliness. He also knew the power of personal integrity and a living faith. It is good news that in a world which brings loneliness there are also resources which bring a sense of fulfillment and the deep conviction that God's creation is good.

3. Satisfaction and Loneliness in Being Oneself

To be oneself involves both satisfaction and loneliness.

In the fourteenth century Meister Eckhart wrote of the satisfaction he found in being himself:

> That I am a man,
> This I share with other men.
> That I see and hear and that I eat and drink
> is what all animals do likewise.
> But that I am I is only mine
> and belongs to me
> and to nobody else; . . .
> not to an angel nor to God—
> except inasmuch as I am one with Him.

In all the history of the universe there has never been and never will be another *I*—"that I am I is only mine." This is indeed an exciting realization. To have one's own unique experience of being human can, indeed, be satisfying.

But to be oneself also involves being shut off in some measure from other persons. Each of us has his or her own center, and in that sense each is alone. Someone has said, "No one else can take your bath for you, no one else can experience your toothache for you, no one else can make your commitment for you, no one else can die your death for you." To be oneself is to experience aloneness. W. H. Auden wrote:

> Aloneness is man's real condition,
> That each must travel forth alone
> In search of the Essential Stone.[1]

The experience of loneliness can go much deeper than just not having another human being to be with at the moment. Sometimes we experience the profound loneliness of being separated from ourselves. In this chapter we shall explore some of the ways in which this takes place. We shall also suggest ways in which we can deal with this form of loneliness.

No two persons are given the gift of life on exactly the same terms. Heredity, cultural influences, environmental factors, and experiences of many kinds combine to make each person's existence different from that of others. Thus, each person has a personal journey to make in self-understanding, in coming to a realization of what his or her life is all about.

In Eugene O'Neill's *Long Day's Journey into Night* the characters move toward a measure of self-understanding. Edmund wrestles with the question of what it means to be a human being. He says:

It was a great mistake, my being born a man, I would have been much more successful as a seagull or a fish. As it is, I will always be a stranger who never feels at home, who does not really want and is not really wanted, who can never belong, who must always be a little in love with death.[2]

So many of the problems in being human revolve around being *this particular* human being. Dwight Moody said, "I have had more trouble with myself than with any other person I ever met." We often have the sense of getting in our own way. We look at other persons and envy them for not having to put up with our problems.

We are learning more and more about the importance of accepting ourselves. Margaret Fuller once said that she had decided to accept the universe. When her friend Thomas Carlyle heard about it he remarked, "Gad, she'd better!" Accepting oneself can be just as important as accepting the universe; in fact, they go hand in hand.

In the midst of our difficulties in self-acceptance we sometimes deny, depreciate, distort, or evade important elements in ourselves. Sometimes we create and live with unrealistic images of ourselves, often created by other people. In the process we do not face up to the realities of our own existence as we might. We may become estranged from ourselves and miss rich possibilities life has for us. The loneliness of self-denial, self-rejection, and self-estrangement is one of the deepest forms of loneliness. We all need a basic self-esteem.

Let us now note some of the dimensions of our real existence from which we sometimes become estranged, but with which we need to come to terms: our past, our bodies, our limitations and aptitudes, our strengths and possibilities, our freedom and responsibilities. Much of the loneliness and much of the meaning in living which we experience revolves around these matters.

Coming to Terms with One's Past

> The Moving Finger writes; and having writ,
> Moves on: nor all your Piety nor Wit
> Shall lure it back to cancel half a Line,
> Nor all your Tears wash out a Word of it.

In these words Omar Khayyám reminds us of one of the exorable conditions of human existence—the irrevocability of the past. What has been done has been done. The experiences we have had with parents and family, the fortunate and unfortunate

53

relationships we have experienced, the successes and failures which have been a part of our lives, the joys and sorrows we have known, are in the lived record and cannot be changed.

What *can* be changed is the meaning these events and experiences have for us. If we wish, we can make a lifelong career of living in the past. We can make some past misfortune or injustice the focal point of our thinking and living. On the other hand, we can draw rich treasures from the past, learn from what we have experienced, and go on to new chapters of life. We are given the gift of life one day at a time and each new day is a new gift.

Some persons are estranged from themselves today because they are preoccupied with reliving their experiences of yesterday. Loneliness is the inevitable result. On the other hand, there are those persons who are open to the goodness, the beauty, and the opportunities which each new day offers to them in their situation.

The sense of being truly alive comes joyfully and meaningfully to those persons who take from the past the values it offers and then go on to affirm each new day. We cannot erase the past, but we can learn from it and we can go beyond it.

Coming to Terms with One's Body

The philosopher Alfred North Whitehead wrote, "Our bodily experience is the basis of our existence. . . . No one ever says, 'Here am I, and I have brought my body with me.'" These words remind us of an elemental truth: we do not simply live in our bodies; rather, we live our bodies. Our personhood, our sense of aliveness, includes our bodily experience.

Yet, multitudes of people experience deep loneliness because they have not really come to terms with their bodies. The acceptance of our body and our self-esteem go hand in hand.

Our bodies are deeply involved in our functioning as persons. We are *externalized* through our bodies; we *communicate* through our bodies; we *learn* through our bodies. Life, mind, and spirit emerge in relation to bodily processes. Biologist Edmund Sinnott wrote, "My contention is not that we should stress the senses against the spirit, but that the body, a necessary portion of our being, should contribute its rightful share not only to our enjoyment, but to the development of the higher levels of life." Our feelings about our bodies and about ourselves as persons are closely related. We live our bodies.

Yet, our bodies pose many problems for us. Many of us experience sickness, or have physical handicaps. Some of us have bodies which are not physically attractive, and others, including many young people, are highly sensitive to what they regard as bodily peculiarities. Our bodies limit us in many ways. We often experience loneliness when we feel excluded from certain relationships and enjoyments by virtue of bodily limitations.

Nevertheless, the body we inhabit is the only one we have—and we must learn to make do with it the best we can. This clearly means that there is not equality of opportunity in the world. Some persons have physical advantages over others. A severely handicapped person once said, "One has the feeling of having to compete against others who have advantages you do not have." There is loneliness reflected in that feeling. But how tragic it is if we recognize our disadvantages, yet fail to find those meanings in life which we can. The person just quoted understood that truth. Helen Keller demonstrated the truth that physical limitations sometimes accompany a radiant spirit. Miss Keller once told how she sometimes yearned that her physical limitations might melt away; but since that could not be, she was determined to use them as tools. If others could be helped thereby, she was happy. When deafness came upon Beethoven he said, "There is no external happiness for you; you must create it for yourself." Many persons are living highly fulfilling lives though physically limited.

Rollo May has observed that self-pity is the one emotion which never did anyone any good. Confronted by physical problems the temptation to give in to self-pity is strong. But that is a road leading to deep loneliness of spirit.

Fortunately, some doors are open to most persons for some joy and meaning in their lives. If our bodies sometimes define limits in terms of which we must live, they also involve us in meaningful relationships with nature, persons, and events. Some of the deepest joys in life involve bodily experience. Too long we have separated body and spirit as though they were in opposition to each other. We need to see persons born to achieve greater wholeness involving both body and spirit. Paul must have had something of this sort in mind when he wrote: "Do you not know that your body is a temple of the Holy Spirit within you, which you have from God? So glorify God in your body" (I Corinthians 6:19, 20).

Coming to Terms with Our Limitations and Aptitudes

This morning I had a conversation with a student who shared with me some of the loneliness he is experiencing. He came to the heart of the problem when he said, "I feel like I am being forced into being someone I am not. Must I keep playing a role not of my own choosing?" Clearly he felt that he was estranged from his real self; he was lonely.

Keeping in touch with our real self involves trying to be realistic about our limitations and aptitudes. We may live in terms of images of ourselves which have little relation to facts. Sometimes we create these images, and sometimes others push them upon us. The result may be frustration, a sense of failure, and separation from our deepest self.

The search for a fulfilling life involves finding a role or roles which we feel to be significant, for which we feel competent, and in which we find satisfaction. Fortunately, there are many human roles to be fulfilled in this world; we do not need to go through life as a carbon copy of someone else.

I have known college and university students who were in school for no better reason than their parents wanted them there and insisted on their attendance. They preferred to be doing something else. On the other hand, I have known young people, hungry for a formal education, who were thrust into situations for which they had no taste whatsoever. Finding roles which are fulfilling for us in the light of our limitations, aptitudes, and interests is important if we are to live with satisfaction.

In a society which places emphasis on position and status it is easy to forget that life is for living and that a truly human existence means more than outdoing or outdistancing someone else. Our basic calling is to fulfill the human role and grow in human qualities within the framework of our own limitations, aptitudes, and possibilities. Robert Browning expressed this idea well in "Bishop Blougram's Apology."

> The common problem, yours, mine, everyone's
> Is—not to fancy what were fair in life
> Provided it could be,—but finding first
> What may be, then find how to make it fair
> Up to our means.

Carl Sandburg wrote of the fish crier on Chicago's Maxwell Street, whose

> face is that of a man terribly glad to be selling fish,
>   terribly glad that
> God made fish, and customers to whom
>   he may call his wares from a pushcart.[3]

It is a beautiful thing to see a person who is "terribly glad" to be fulfilling a useful role in home, school, office, shop, factory, farm, legislative hall, or anywhere else. That sort of gladness involves the recognition that "life is the art of the possible," and each of us needs to come to terms with our particular limitations and aptitudes. Success is not simply a matter of external achievement; it includes the sense of satisfaction in being true to our real self in responsible relationship to others.

In a society in which widespread unemployment is a fact and desired opportunities are not open to us, the problem of finding fulfilling roles is often difficult. But the basic point remains—failure to come to terms with our limitations and aptitudes leads to self-estrangement and loneliness. To affirm life as the art of the possible is to move toward fulfillment as a person of worth and integrity.

Keeping in Touch with Our Capacities and Strengths

"I believe that we have not even begun to tap human potentialities."

"Perhaps the greatest lesson which anthropology can teach is that of the boundless plasticity of 'human nature.'"

"An attitude becoming a thoughtful, scientifically oriented student of nature is one of gratitude for the richness of its apparent potentialities."

These statements come from distinguished persons who have spent years dealing with human beings: anthropologists Margaret Mead and Clyde Kluckhohn, and Gardner Murphy, the former Director of Research at the Menninger Foundation. It is significant that persons such as these emerge with essentially positive and hopeful views of the human creature.

How easy it is to fall prey to inadequate images of ourselves. Because someone in our past did not expect much of us, or because of some failure along the way, we may be selling ourselves short. There is a loneliness which attends being estranged from our own capacities and strengths. Most of us have more capacity for coping, for growing, for discovering, for overcoming, for meaning something to someone else, for taking some worthwhile next step than we suppose.

A businessman read an article entitled "You, Too,

Can Paint." He took up the challenge, enrolled in an art class, and soon was painting. In astonishment he said to a friend, "I didn't know I had it in me!" And he would never have known it if he had not tried.

Abraham Maslow has reminded us that two kinds of motives operate within us. One, he calls "deficit motives," which are directed to the reduction of tension. Then, there are "growth motives," which are directed toward the achievement of goals. When we settle back in the interest of comfort into the path of least resistance, we are moving with the deficit motives. When we do some stretching of mind, body, or spirit in the interest of some new experience, some creative enterprise, or some potential relationship of meaning we are moving with the growth motives. Both motives have their rightful place, but to yield to the deficit motives is to become estranged from something terribly important in ourselves—our strengths and capacities for greater aliveness.

There is nothing more deadly than boredom—the sense that there is nothing new under the sun, nothing to be excited about. Boredom is related to loneliness. On the other hand, there is nothing more renewing than the satisfaction of being linked with the processes of creation in work, in play, in human relations, in hobbies, in coping with problems, in sensitivity to those points in our environment where life is struggling to spring forth. In her book *Our Inner Conflicts* Karen Horney insisted that "all of us retain the capacity to change, even to change in fundamental ways, as long as we live." The possibility of changed attitudes, changed situations, changed appreciations, and changed relationships belong to those who do not become estranged from their own capacities and strengths. They are the persons who possess a major resource against emptiness and loneliness of spirit.

Meeting Loneliness Head-On by Exercising Our Freedom and Responsibility

Recently I witnessed a beautiful drama on the shore of Maroon Lake near Aspen, Colorado. A little girl timidly climbed out on a fallen tree which extended several feet into the shallow water. At one point she slipped and fell into the water. Although the water was no more than a few inches deep at that point, the child was badly frightened and began crying. Her father, who was standing by watching the procedure, came to her rescue and comforted her. After a few moments he said quietly, "Wouldn't you like to try it again?" She was not at all sure of that—it was a frightening venture. But with some encouragement from her father, she made the decision. This time she made it to the end of the tree trunk and all the way back to shore where there was a happy reunion. She and her father then walked away—hand in hand—joyous in the decision which had been made and in the victory which had been won. I was fortunate enough to get a picture of the little girl just as she was finishing her successful venture. That picture will always be a reminder to me of the importance and wonder of the gift of decision which has been given to us. A little child shall lead them . . .

The freedom to make significant decisions is an important part of each of us. The responsibility to make those decisions in the awareness that our lives are linked with other lives is essential in achieving a truly human existence. Through the exercise of freedom and responsibility we come to heightened self-esteem and to greater satisfaction in being who we are. Loneliness has less of a grip upon us so long as we are exercising responsible freedom.

In his book *Escape from Freedom* Erich Fromm has reminded us of some of the ways in which we endeavor to avoid the effort and pain of exercising mature freedom. In Franz Kafka's *Castle* we meet a man who spends a lifetime trying to get in touch with the mysterious inhabitants of a castle who will tell him what to do and make decisions for him. He fails in his attempts and comes to the end of life with a sense of futility and loneliness. Sometimes we avoid the responsibility of decision by pretending that our fate is determined by something that happened in the past or by what is written in the stars. We often yield to immature dependencies on authority figures and/or groups. Sometimes we resign our personal identities through a life-style of conforming to the crowd or going the way the wind is blowing. Loneliness is one of the prices of making decisions, but there is a deeper and more tragic loneliness in making no decisions at all.

Day-by-day decisions concerning our attitudes, our responses to situations, our priorities, our stand on issues, and our readiness to assume certain responsibilities and challenges may seem rather insignificant in themselves, but together they add up to a great deal. W. E. Hocking reminded us that a slight shift in the set of the ship's rudder at the outset of a voyage makes a great difference in the point of arrival. So it is in the journey of life—the day-by-day exercise of freedom for decision-making has much to do with what meaning life has for us. To avoid the exercise of freedom and responsibility is to deny something profoundly real in ourselves and invite loneliness of spirit.

Someone remarked that astronomically speaking, the human creature is insignifcant. To which someone else replied, "Astronomically speaking, the human creature *is* the astronomer." In a world which seems so vast, our decisions are more important than we know.

Summary

In this chapter we have considered the deep loneliness and emptiness of spirit we experience when we are separated from the sources of renewal within ourselves. This isolation is compounded when we fall into self-rejection and self-depreciation. To come to terms with our past, our bodies, our limitations and aptitudes, our strengths and possibilities, and our freedom and responsibilities in creative ways is to move toward fulfillment of life; to be out of touch with them is to experience profound loneliness.

Under these circumstances each one of us has a basic decision to make: do we accept the gift of life on the terms it is offered to us, given our limitations and capacities? If not, we inevitably move toward a life of self-rejection, self-pity, bitterness, and loneliness. If we inwardly affirm the gift of life, we have many problems to deal with, but we also experience in a growing way the wonder and meaning of a truly human existence.

Ralph Waldo Emerson stated this very well in his essay on self-reliance.

There is a time in every man's education when he arrives at the conviction that envy is ignorance; that imitation is suicide; that he must take himself for better, for worse, as his portion; that though the wide universe is full of good, no kernel of nourishing corn can come to him but through his toil bestowed on that plot of ground which is given to him to till.

That is a wisdom we all need if we are to be educated in the art of meaningful living.

4. When Separation and Isolation Bring Loneliness

In this chapter we shall consider the deep loneliness which attends separation and isolation. Specifically, we shall consider unfulfilled longings for an understanding person or persons to talk to, the aloneness which accompanies being the victim of discrimination and prejudice, and the loneliness experienced in sickness and dying. In considering these matters we shall be dealing with some of the most painful forms of loneliness—forms which often go unrecognized by other persons.

Unfulfilled Longings for Communication with an Understanding Person

"I'm so lonely I could die. So alone, I cannot write. My hands and fingers pain me. I see no human beings. My phone never rings ... I hear from no one ... Never had any kind of holidays, no kind. My birthday is this month ... Isn't anyone else lonely like me? ... I don't know what to do."

These words were written by an eighty-four-year-old woman living in a rundown apartment building in Los Angeles. She sent this message to *The Los Angeles Times*. She also enclosed some stamps in the hope that someone might write to her, and a one-dollar bill so that someone might telephone her. "Will someone call me?" she pleaded. When a newspaper reporter did call, she broke into tears. "If you are alone you die every day," she said. "I just eat and sleep. Sometimes I just dread to see myself wake up in the morning."

This elderly woman was experiencing separation and isolation; she was both alone and lonely. Most of all, she wanted someone she could talk to, share experiences with, and be understood by. Regardless of age we all need that. Ina May Greer has written:

> Most of us seem to need someone to scold us a little, reassure us, listen to us, baby us, even spat a little with us well within the bounds of safety and so help us drain off our accumulating tension. And, this is very important, we need someone against whom we can test our thinking and check our insights. For too many in our era there is no one to take over the friendly and family functions of support, correction, teasing, admiration indulgence, affection, and to offer a safe, because understanding and loving, outlet for our minor irritations. Most of us need someone to help us heal after an emotional stress or conquer our gains by letting us talk them out. . . . We need people we like and who like us, and we need them to be near enough to be talked to and looked at occasionally.[1]

Persons of all ages find themselves in situations where there is a minimum opportunity for such communication and companionship. Sometimes the opportunities are there, but they have not been utilized. Individuals uprooted from smaller communities where they were known and cared about, single persons living alone—sometimes following divorce, young mothers in situations providing a minimum of outlet beyond the home, and many others are subject to the loneliness of having no understanding person at hand with whom they can communicate about the things which really matter to them. It is reported that thousands of telephone calls are placed each day to numbers offering a message of some sort—including the temperature or time of day—just to hear a human voice speaking to them.

There is no substitute for communication with an

<u>understanding person.</u> When one finds oneself in a situation where opportunity for such communication is minimal, there are several things which can be done, although none takes the place of what is most yearned for. One can use such opportunities for friendly talk as are available. The elderly woman in Los Angeles told of talking to the man who cashed her Social Security check, and to children near her apartment. One can ask, "Is there *anything* I can do to relate to someone somewhere?" This same isolated woman in Los Angeles made the effort to write a letter in the hope of establishing some sort of communication. Except in cases of near helplessness, most persons can do something to reach out to someone else, to take some first step in establishing communication. There are many other lonely persons in the world. In most communities there are interest groups of varied kinds which bring persons together. Increasingly, churches provide resources for persons to come together in small communities or groups for fellowship, for learning, and for serving.

Every human being needs to feel some kinship with the nonhuman world about him. One needs growing things close at hand, some form of life, and a window to the outside world.

Regardless of how many persons one has to talk to, we all still need an inner life nourished by books and music, things of beauty, and pictures which remind us of persons and places with whom we have associations of memory and love. Confined to her home and bed for a long period of illness, Louisa Alcott was asked, "How can you stand it?" To which she replied, "I enjoy my mind." The fact that we are experiencing solitude does not necessarily mean that we are completely alone.

The Loneliness of Prejudice and Discrimination

In recent years we have witnessed the rise of various liberation movements based on race, sex, economic status, and so forth. Sometimes we fail to recognize that behind these movements is a deep loneliness in the lives of persons being discriminated against or in some way set apart.

Those of us who are identified with majority groups often find it difficult to understand the pain and heartache which goes with being pushed aside or denied basic human rights because of race, sex, nationality, and so on.

Abraham Maslow told of being the only Jewish boy in a non-Jewish Brooklyn suburb. He wrote, "I was isolated and unhappy. I grew up in libraries and among books, almost without friends."

In 1963 Martin Luther King, Jr. spoke of the loneliness and pain of a child learning the fact of discrimination:

> When you suddenly find your tongue twisted and your speech stammering as you seek to explain to your six-year-old daughter why she can't go to the amusement park that has just been advertised on television, and see tears welling up in her little eyes; when she is told "Funtown" is closed to colored children, and you see the depressing clouds of inferiority begin to form in her little mental sky, and see her begin to distort her little personality by unconsciously developing a bitterness toward white people .... when you are forever fighting a sense of "nobodyness"—then you will understand why we find it difficult to wait.[2]

Fortunately, significant advances in civil rights have been made since those words were spoken, but race prejudice is still very much with us, accompanied by loneliness in the lives of those who are discriminated against.

The documentary film *Antonia: A Portrait Of The Woman* depicts the struggle of Antonia Brico, a symphony orchestra conductor, to find acceptance in a field dominated by men. In a moving scene with Judy Collins, Dr. Brico pours out the heartache she endured through many years. Now in her seventies, she is belatedly receiving invitations to conduct major orchestras throughout the world—in part because of the influence of this film. A few evenings ago I heard her say, "The hurt is over." But for multitudes of persons less favored, the hurt continues.

In our society there are other persons who feel the pain of isolation and rejection for different reasons. Recently increasing attention has been given to homosexuality and the problems of the homosexual. *Time* magazine ran a cover story on September 8, 1975 entitled, "I Am a Homosexual: The Gay Drive for Acceptance." In government, business, church, and many other segments of our society, issues related to homosexuality are being debated; and behind the scenes thousands of homosexuals are experiencing loneliness.

Many other different segments of our society might be mentioned as we consider the plight of persons experiencing the loneliness of discrimination and prejudice. It is a hopeful sign that increasing attention is being given to our penal system. It can hardly be debated that crimes are committed in the name of justice. Among the problems requiring more attention is the plight of the individual who has been estranged from the law, has been imprisoned, and now is seeking a new life in society. It hardly needs to be said that profound loneliness is being experienced by many such individuals. The way is not easy. These words written by Winston Churchill are worth pondering:

> The mood and temper of the public with regard to the treatment of crime and criminals is one of the most unfailing tests of the civilization of any country. A calm, dispassionate recognition of the rights of the accused, and even of the convicted criminal against the state; a constant heart-searching by all charged with the duty of punishment; a desire and an eagerness to rehabilitate; . . . tireless efforts toward the discovery of creative and regenerative processes; unfailing faith that there is a treasure, if only you can find it, in the heart of every man. These are the symbols which . . . mark and measure the stored-up strength of a nation . . . proof of the living virtue in it.[3]

All of us find it easier to recognize and identify with problems similar to our own. We too often forget that all around us are persons experiencing forms of loneliness which are foreign to us. In the midst of our own experiences of loneliness it is well to think of other persons also. Sometimes our own loneliness is alleviated as we try to reach out to that of another. As citizens, we need to be concerned about those conditions in our society which make it difficult for many deserving persons to enjoy acceptance, understanding, and the full rights of citizenship.

The Experience of Being Sick

Sooner or later we all experience sickness.

Many books and articles have been written on care of the sick and ministering to the sick, but surprisingly little has been written on the actual experience of being sick. We are now concerned with loneliness as a part of the experience of illness.

Pain, fatigue, anxiety, and worries about family, work, the future, and finances often attend the experience of sickness. When the fact of one's illness really dawns on a person, he or she is likely to have the sense of separation from so many of the persons and things which are part of his usual life. There is strangeness in illness which often leads to loneliness.

Whenever illness comes it represents an interruption in our life. Things just cannot go on as usual. Our pattern of life is disturbed; things we had planned to do must be postponed or given up. Sickness seems to be a great intruder. Fortunate, indeed, is that person who has reflected seriously enough on the ways of things to recognize that some interruptions are inevitable. We all need a philosophy of life which in some measure helps us make our peace with the fundamental way of things.

Human beings experience illness under many different circumstances. There are the short illnesses of a few days in which we are confined to our homes. There are illnesses which involve hospitalization and possibly surgery. In the midst of strange persons and noises and unfamiliar procedures—separated from one's usual surroundings—one is very likely to experience loneliness. There are illnesses involving long periods of convalescence. Sometimes one must face up to the fact that he or she will be permanently limited or handicapped in some way. There are the long illnesses in which the outcome is not certain.

Most of us cannot know ahead of time just how we will respond to the experience of a serious illness. This is, indeed, one of the testing times of life. Simple answers or admonitions are out of place. But as we contemplate the possibility of future illness, or as we reflect on illness we now are experiencing, there are several things which can be said.

In illness there are support systems to which we can turn. To be open to these resources is important. Amazing advances have been made in the medical sciences in recent years. The medical profession is a helping profession. There are resources both scientific and personal in the physician-patient relationship.

A modern hospital is an amazing support community. We most readily see the physician and nurses, but behind the scene are hundreds of persons providing various services for the sick. A plaque on Denver General Hospital reads:

Dedicated to the People of Denver As a Center for Health Care, So That They May Find Ready Help in Time of Need in an Atmosphere of Enlightenment and Kindness . . . A Place Where Life Begins and Well-Being Is Fostered; Where Crisis Is Met and Life Is Celebrated.

The inner resources which we bring to the experience of sickness are so very important. To have persons, places, and experiences which strengthen us in our thinking about them, to be responsive to touches of kindness and beauty close at hand, to be able to relate to a flower or a growing plant, to be able to read and listen to music and be enriched thereby, to be able to turn our thoughts outward to other persons in need, to be able to exercise our imagination in relation to the future— is to have resources of the spirit in the midst of illness. With these, we are not wholly alone.

But most important of all in the realm of spiritual

undergirding is a religious faith. He who prays knows that he is not alone. He who prays affirms a wisdom, a presence, a grace and a love which is more than a human wisdom, presence, grace, and love. Religious faith is the ultimate resource in dealing with loneliness.

I first met Janice Sinclair in 1968 when she was at Fitzsimmons General Hospital in Denver as Staff Dietician. Shortly thereafter she accepted an assignment on the staff of a church-related hospital in South America. Her work in this new situation was getting underway meaningfully when she was diagnosed as having Hodgkin's disease. The years since have brought suffering and uncertainty about the future. She now lives with her parents in Gregory, South Dakota. A letter dated July 6, 1975 says:

It is meaningful to me to feel some physical renewal developing, though slowly after a long and crushing winter . . . . In reality I am a shut-in, as my activities are pretty well limited by lack of stamina and strength. The challenge lies for me in continuing to be involved in what is happening around me, being truly sensitive to it all—and growing intellectually, emotionally, and spiritually. I think this is really important and I am committted to it as well as to the business of being about what I am to be about with my life in Christ as a whole, in view of the limitations. I still hope for the opportunity for direct involvement in a study/work situation in a public health situation with emphasis on nutrition, of course. I anticipate and prepare for this though I certainly don't know when it will at last become possible. For the present I concentrate as heartily as possible on the present, day by day feeling relieved that the months of summer stretch ahead. . . . that is the essence of my report to you!

Loneliness in suffering and sickness is a fact, sometimes seemingly unbearable. But persons like Jan Sinclair help us to understand the reality and greatness of the human spirit. And beyond that— the reality of God.

Loneliness in Terminal Illness and in Dying

The human being experiencing terminal illness is a real person with thoughts, feelings, and concerns. It is a tragic fact that in our death-denying, death-evading culture we too often lose sight of this central fact. The dying person is frequently neglected, put aside, abandoned. We need to give much more attention to the experience of dying both as an individual and social fact: family, friends, the medical team, and the community are all involved. Dying, in the sense that we are using the word, may involve many months of moving toward death in a terminal illness.

It is inevitable that loneliness should attend the experience of dying. Every individual dies his own death and is alone in that experience. In an insightful article Dr. E. Mansell Pattison has identified seven fears which are likely to attend the experience of dying: fear of the unknown, fear of loneliness, fear of loss of family and friends, fear of loss of body, fear of loss of self-control, fear of loss of identity, and fear of regression. He points out that the dying person need not be completely alone in dealing with these fears, provided there are understanding persons *to be with him.* He writes:

If the dying person is provided the opportunity and assistance, then the experience of dying can be a part of living .... Although we cannot deal with the ultimate problem of death, we can help the person to deal with the various parts of the process of dying. ... Only when the clinician has come to face death within himself can he begin to practice the high therapeutic art of helping people to die.[4]

A basic change in our attitudes toward dying is required if we are to deal with loneliness in terminal illness on a level of depth. Terminal illness is regarded too frequently as simply a matter of "waiting for the end." What is often missed is the truth that dying is one aspect of the whole human career. It has its distinctive meanings within the framework of the life-death cycle. Insofar as the patient is in possession of mental faculties with the power of reflection, there are things to be accomplished in and through the dying processes, things of deep human significance. Incredible as it may seem to some persons, there is a type of personal fulfillment to be found in death which is related to achievements experienced in the preceding chapters of life.

In her book *On Death and Dying* Elisabeth Kübler-Ross identifies five stages in the dying process: denial and isolation, anger, bargaining, depression, and acceptance. Dr. Kübler-Ross points out how natural it is that the dying patient should experience deep and often conflicting feelings. But all of this may be involved in working through to the awareness that something important and significant is happening in one's dying. The dying patient may resign himself to a meaningless end of existence. On the other hand, having lived through the stages of dying with a sense of identity and integrity, the patient may "affirm death as the natural fulfillment of life and completion of its meaning and purpose."[5]

To be able to say and to feel that one's own life is finished is a part of life's meaning. The record has been written. The journey has been made. This is how a person discovers who he is.

Stewart Alsop, distinguished author and journalist, learned at the age of fifty-seven that he was possibly near the end of his life. He spoke of the "appalling loneliness" he experienced when he faced the facts in his situation. But his last days and months were not a time simply of waiting for the end. He reflected both on past and future, he assessed his own life, and he lived through the experience with a sense of identity and integrity. In his journal *Stay of Execution* he wrote:

No experience has been more interesting than living in intermittent intimacy with the gentleman W. C. Fields used to call "the man in the white nightgown" and whom I have come to think of as Uncle Thanatos, and sometimes, when I have been feeling very sick, as dear old Uncle Thanatos.[6]

Stewart Alsop lived while he was dying.

Writing out of a different philosophical viewpoint Pierre Teilhard de Chardin reflected on the experience of dying. He thought of dying as entrance into a new relationship with God. He put his thoughts and hopes in the form of prayer:

Bring me to a serene acceptance of that final phase of communion with you in which I shall attain to possession of you by diminishing within you.

Grant me, then, something even more precious than that grace for which all your faithful followers pray: to receive communion as I die is not sufficient: *teach me to make a communion of death itself.*[7]

The experience of dying may bring with it the affirmation of our own selfhood and integrity. It may also bring the undergirding trust that in walking through the valley of the shadow of death, we are not alone.

5. Loneliness in the Experience of Grief

In an article "A Loneliness I Never Expected" published in *The New York Times*, Ralph Cokain told of his personal experience of loneliness in grief. He wrote:

We had shared so many years together, we had shared so many wonderful and exciting experiences, we were so much in love and such inseparable companions, the very idea that one of us would die and leave the other alone and bereaved seemed so remotely distant that we refused to entertain it and spoil our fun.

But death did come unexpectedly—and with it loneliness.

Come the first day of summer (what irony!) she will have been dead two years.

I miss her terribly and I have agonized—nearly to the point of self-destruction.

I am living a loneliness I never expected. I feel so vulnerable, so inferior, so unsure of myself.

I find no purpose in living, though I have been told that purpose will eventually manifest itself. There are no fond expectations, no stimulating goals, no promising future.

Everything seems different—even the newspaper she loved so much and the newsmagazine that could disturb her routine if it arrived a day late. We frequented so many places I am constantly reminded of her; the music we shared I cannot bear to hear now. What anguish to come home night after night to an apartment devoid of her warmth and radiance.[1]

Anyone who has experienced grief can understand the pain behind those words, for grief is the price of love.

The circumstances under which grief is experienced vary in the lives of different persons. But under any circumstances the marks of grief go deep. To deny the pain of grief is to live a lie.

In the death of someone we have loved something of ourselves dies, too. Love is a relationship; in death that relationship is changed, and in some sense broken. We share in the dying. Ralph Barton Perry wrote, "Those with whom we live become inextricably interwoven with the whole fabric of our lives. If we love people we live in them, and if they die something of us dies too." Upon the death of one close to him George Santayana wrote, "With you a part of me hath passed away."

The whole person grieves. Body, mind, and spirit are involved. It is no wonder that after the initial shock and numbness, one should possibly experience nervousness, insomnia, trembling, loss of appetite, tightness in the throat, shortness of breath.

Although no two persons grieve precisely alike, it is not uncommon for grieving persons to experience feelings of helplessness and hopelessness, anger, guilt, depression, the desire to search for the deceased, sharp pangs of grief, or a sense of panic. The grieving person sometimes condemns himself or herself for "not doing better." One of the significant recent studies of bereavement and grief includes this statement:

Many bereaved people are surprised and frightened by the sheer intensity of their emotions and imaginings after bereavement . . . . Bereaved people are so surprised by the unaccustomed feelings of grief that they often ask, "Am I going mad?" or "Is it normal to be like this?" Such fears are particularly felt when intense feelings of anger or bitterness erupt, but they may also arise in relation to disturbances of perception . . . Distractability, difficulty in remembering everyday matters, and a slight sense of unreality are other features of the typical reaction to bereavement which may worry the bereaved. There is no reason to regard any of these as signs of mental illness.[2]

Grief experiences vary in a number of respects. There is reason to believe that survivors of persons who have died unexpectedly and suddenly may experience more intense and lasting grief than those who have had time in which to make some inner preparation for bereavement. Colin Murray Parkes has written of variations in experience:

Those who are concerned with the effects of bereavement have to take into consideration many possible factors when trying to explain the differences between individuals in their response to this event. It is not enough to say that the loss of a love object causes grief, and leave it at that. Grief may be strong or weak, brief or prolonged, immediate or delayed; particular aspects of it may be distorted and symptoms that usually cause little trouble may become sources of major distress.[3]

Unfortunately there are some persons who like to think of themselves as being "too strong to grieve" or as having a philosophy or religious faith that makes them "above" experiencing grief. The experience of grief, in all its pain and loneliness, is not a sign of weakness. It is a mark of being human.

Grief Has Its Work To Do

When one is experiencing the first sharp pains and deep loneliness of loss and grief he is not yet ready to reflect on the important truth that grief has its work to do. There are hours when one's task is simply to endure what must be endured, to do what must now be done.

But later there come those hours when hopefully it is given us to know that grief is not without meaning and purpose. If grief is, indeed, the price of love, it is one phase of the larger process of affirming that love, and building it into new chapters of life. The death of a loved one calls for an inner reorientation, the fashioning of a new identity in a world of meaning.

Somewhere in the grieving process one makes a basic decision: to cling simply to the past and mourn without hope, or to live through the experience of grief drawing from its very depths the wisdom and strength to go on and to affirm a new and meaningful chapter of life. Fortunately, there are resources to help us. One way to affirm the love of one who has died is to plant it like a seed in a garden, that it might flower in new ways in new days in new relationships.

There is no timetable for the experience of grief. It is important to be gentle with ourselves, at the same time recognizing that our own attitudes have something to do in determining whether there is to be healing through grieving. The loved one who has died is not going to be restored to us. A part of our need is to adjust to a new set of circumstances—but more than adjustment is involved. Certain things need to happen within ourselves as we come to participate in a new environment and a new pattern of life.

There are three important phases or steps involved in healing grief. We cannot put these on a precise timetable because they sometimes overlap. We may feel that we are regressing rather than going forward. We cannot force the movement in these steps, but we can be open to and cooperate with the healing reality which works through these phases. As with a physical wound, there are some things we can do; but we cannot do everything. Fortunately, there is a healing reality ready to work in us and through us—silently and gradually. The three kinds of work to be accomplished through grief might be referred to as the *expressing, adjusting,* and *re-creating* phases of grief.

Our feelings need to be acknowledged and expressed in some way. The attempt to deny our painful and mixed feelings, to put a lid on them, and to act as if we suppress them they will go away will not work. It is important that our feelings be permitted to emerge into consciousness. Precisely how they are expressed varies with each of us, but they do need to be acknowledged and expressed. Some weeks after his wife died, a friend wrote a letter including these words.

"For everything there is a season . . . a time to be born and a time to die." I can understand the reality of the thought, but can't seemingly reconcile myself to the permanency of the separation. To me [she] is still as near, but invisible, to me as ever—it is so hard to keep waiting for the day this grief will relent, but equally difficult to consider the loss, if ever it does, of her not being so near and so much a part of me.

Sometimes several hours may pass without her presence and then suddenly for an almost unidentifiable reason she envelops my emotions and I must stop what I'm doing, excuse myself, if I can control my voice, and abruptly leave an appointment, or even rise and walk out of a staff meeting or other gathering without an explanation . . . . I do feel a bit relieved now that I've put down a few thoughts.

To express some of our feelings, whether in conversation with one person, in a group, or in some other way is to know that we are not entirely alone, even in the midst of a sense of desolation. The expressing phase of grief has its work to do. In *Macbeth* Shakespeare advised:

Give sorrow words; the grief that does not speak
Whispers the o'er-fraught heart and bids it break.

The adjusting phase of grief involves facing the fact that our world has changed and there is no going back to what has been. I heard of a woman who, a year after her husband's death, continued to set a place for him at the table and arrange his chair the way he liked to have it. She was engaging in a form of denial. She could not bring herself to say, "My husband has died. Things will not be as they were. I must do my living in a changed environment and a changed world. Indeed, I must be in touch with myself in a new way. I must begin to fashion a new image of myself." The adjusting phase of grief includes reflection on a changed pattern of life. It brings forth the slow emergence of some sense of getting things sorted out a bit—a pattern, a schedule, a possible way of existing under changed conditions.

The re-creating phase of grief involves the first steps of reaching out, taking a first step or steps into a world where one is alone in a way he or she was not alone before, affirming one's selfhood, taking the risk of trusting life to give us something of what we need. Gradually it may come to us that some things of importance have been happening in ourselves. We see some things we had not seen this way before. We feel some things in a different way. Perhaps we are a bit more understanding of the hurts of others. Yes, it may be that we have something to give which we did not have to give before. It is not just a matter of adjusting to what must be. It is also a matter of helping to create something of worth and meaning which *might be*. Healing is in that person who can say, "Even though I have experienced the depths, I have survived, and I am alive."

The book of Ecclesiastes reminds us that "For everything there is a season . . . a time to be born, and a time to die" (3:1,2). It also reminds us that "he who is joined with all the living has hope" (9:4). After the loss of a loved one, it is sometimes difficult to leave our solitude and venture into a new and changed world. But in taking that step we sometimes discover that there are resources of strength and healing in the very situations we had avoided or feared. To be joined with the living brings perspective, support, and hope.

Life is never the same again after the death of a loved one. There is loneliness. But to grieve creatively, through expressing, adjusting, and re-creating, is to change the meaning of our loneliness. Out of the heart of loneliness there sometimes comes deepened self-understanding, greater sensitivity to others and their needs, and the discovery that even in solitude we are not alone.

Companions on the Journey Through Grief

In the midst of grief the sense of our aloneness can be overwhelming. But deep within us and around us are resources which we may not recognize for a time and may feel unable to relate to. But they are there, and we are less alone than we realize. If we will have it so, there are companions on the journey through grief available to us. At first, it may seem strange to think of these resources as "companions," but they can be that. Even in our aloneness we need not be completely alone. Let us consider, then, the companionship of memory, of the inner presence of the one we have loved, of other human beings, of God. Insofar as these resources do become companions through grief we shall discover that there are turning points on the journey—and those turning points are toward healing and hope.

The Companionship of Memory. William Allen White, longtime distinguished editor of the Emporia, Kansas *Gazette,* wrote of the sorrow he and his wife experienced in the death of their seventeen-year-old daughter. He spoke also of the profound gratitude they felt for the privilege of having had her as a daughter. Their memories of her were companions on their journey through grief. He wrote:

Mrs. White and I have none but joyous memories of Mary. She gave out humor and sunshine as beaten steel gives out sparks, and all our recollections of her are merry ones . . . . Her loss was a terrible blow yet we are not dubious of God or the decency of man . . . . Mary is a net gain. To have had her for seventeen years, joyous and rollicking and wise and so tremendously human in her weakness and in her strength is blessing enough for any parents and we have no right to ask for more.[4]

There is healing in recalling—and sharing with someone else—specific things about the loved one who has died. To remember things said and done, experiences shared and places visited, seemingly little events which one treasures, worthwhile things accomplished, and influences that live on, is to experience memory as a good companion. We honor one who has died by recalling characteristic things about him or her. Some of these memories can and should be shared with others. Some we treasure privately. Henry Wadsworth Longfellow wrote of this in his poem "Holidays."

> The holiest of all holidays are those
> Kept by ourselves in silence and apart;
> The secret anniversaries of the heart.

Helen Hayes has told of the agony she experienced following the death of her daughter with polio. A family who had lost their son with polio came to call. Miss Hayes writes:

Mrs. Frantz soon began talking about her son in a most natural manner, and, before I quite knew what was happening, I had plunged into a series of stories about Mary. Then a glance at Charles' surprised face made me realize that I was actually mentioning her name for the first time since her death. I had taken her memory out of hiding, and I felt better for it.[5]

Memories may remind us of how great our loss is. By the same token, they may remind us of how greatly we have been blessed. To affirm and share our memories is to affirm our loved one. It is also to move toward a healing of spirit.

The Companionship of the Inner Presence of the Loved One. Many persons experiencing grief report sensing the presence of the one who has died. As one woman put it, "It seems as though he is here with me." My friend, whom I quoted earlier said, "To me [she] is still as near, but invisible, to me as ever." How natural it is that it should be so. When lives are deeply interrelated death cannot quickly terminate the feeling of the near presence of the other.

With the passage of time the sense of the influence of the one who has died may take on a somewhat different form. One becomes increasingly aware of how much the other person has contributed—and continues to contribute—to one's own selfhood. In speaking of a person who had died Browning wrote, "Death has done all death can." As time goes on one realizes that there are some things death cannot do. Death cannot stop the outreaching influence of a life, nor can death take away what one has contributed to the life of another.

Mr. and Mrs. John Gunther were parents of a seventeen-year-old son who died of a brain tumor. Out of this experience both parents put some thoughts and feelings into writing. In his moving memoir *Death Be Not Proud* Mr. Gunther wrote:

> We said goodbye. But to anybody who ever knew him, he is still alive. I do not mean merely that he lives in both of us or in the trees at Deerfield or in anything he touched truly, but that the influence, the impact, of a heroic personality continues to exert itself long after the mortal bonds are snapped. Johnny transmits permanently something of what he was, since the fabric of the universe is continuous and eternal.[6]

Mrs. Gunther agreed with her husband that "Johnny transmits permanently something of what he was." She found strength and purpose in the growing awareness that she herself could be an instrument of what was best in Johnny's life. She wrote:

> I wish we had loved Johnny more when he was alive. Of course we loved Johnny very much. Johnny knew that. Everybody knew it. Loving Johnny more. What does it mean? What can it mean now?
>
> Parents all over the world who lost sons in the war have felt this kind of question, and sought an answer.
>
> To me, it means loving life more, being more aware of life, of one's fellow human beings, of the earth.
>
> It means obliterating, in a curious but real way, the ideas of evil and hate and the enemy, and transmuting them, with the alchemy of suffering, into ideas of clarity and charity.
>
> It means caring more and more about other people, at home and abroad, all over the earth. It means caring more about God.
>
> I hope we can love Johnny more and more till we, too, die, and leave behind us, as he did the love of love, the love of life.[7]

When our thoughts begin turning outward in this kind of love for the one who has died, grief is doing its work.

The Companionship of Other Human Beings.
Helen Keller is reported to have said that if one has
a friend, he can stand anything. Blessed are those
who on their journey through grief are able to draw
on the strength which is given by other human
beings. In the grieving processes there are times
when one wants to be alone; such times are
needed. But continuing withdrawal is not good; one
needs what only other human beings can give.

Because our situations differ we vary in the
number of human beings who are available to us.
Some individuals are very much alone with a
minimum of human contacts. Others are more
fortunate. Among those who may be available are
these: family and close friends; acquaintances in
neighborhood and other associations; minister,
priest, or rabbi; persons we have not met, but who
make their presence known. Each of these persons
is a reminder that even in our loneliness we have
bonds of support and linkages of meaning.

To have family and/or close friends with whom to
share our grief is to be blessed. So many experiences have been shared that words are scarcely
needed. By their presence family and close friends
remind us that we are not entirely alone. We have
precious linkages of understanding and support.

Beyond the circle of family and our closest
friends are other friends and acquaintances. In
their coming to us in a time of grief we are
reminded not only of their caring, but of our
relationship to a neighborhood and a community.

If one is related to a religious heritage and is
affiliated with church or synagogue, he has resources available which go deep. Persons with
whom we have been associated in worship and

work, sharing and serving help to communicate a faith which is rooted in centuries of living. Our spiritual counsellor—be he minister, priest, or rabbi—comes as a trusted friend. He also comes as a representative of our community of faith. He brings the resources of faith sometimes expressed in scripture, prayer, and sacrament. He helps us to draw on our own inner spiritual resources which we may have forgotten were there.

In the midst of grief a word, a note, a call often comes from someone we have not seen or heard from in many years. Sometimes a message comes from someone we have never met before, but who wishes to express concern. Such communications remind us that we are not as much alone as we had thought. There are invisible bonds which become real to us when needed most. Such human linkages are companions on our journey through grief. It is for us to be open to human expressions of concern as are available to us. For most people there are more resources available than we had supposed while in the depths of sorrow.

God the Companion in Grief. Out of the experience of grief and suffering and testing have come many testimonies of God's sustaining presence and companionship. The psalmist said, "My flesh and my heart may fail, but God is the strength of my heart and my portion forever" (Psalm 73:26). "Even though I walk through the valley of the shadow of death, I fear no evil; for thou art with me" (Psalm 23:4). Many persons have found renewal of spirit in the words from the sixty-first chapter of Isaiah: "The Spirit of the Lord God is upon me, because the LORD has anointed me to bring good tidings to the afflicted; he has sent me to bind up the brokenhearted, . . . to comfort all who mourn, . . . to grant to those who mourn in Zion . . . the oil of gladness instead of mourning, the mantle of praise instead of a faint spirit" (Isaiah 61:1,2,3). The Gospel of John which has so much to say about the indwelling spirit of God affirms, "Peace I leave with you; my peace I give to you; not as the world gives do I give to you. Let not your hearts be troubled, neither let them be afraid" (John 14:27).

Through the centuries and in our own day many persons have found these biblical affirmations confirmed in their own experience. I think of the young man whose young wife died suddenly. Unashamedly he poured out his grief and then said, "But I believe in God." I think of a man in his late eighties who had lived through so much and who had survived so much. Upon the death of his wife—his good companion for almost sixty years—he expressed his grief, his appreciation for her life, and his faith. He spoke simply, "It is a heavy burden to bear—but not too great for friendship and for faith."

Persons may express their trust in God in different ways. There is no one way to express it. At the heart of it is the deep conviction that even in one's grief and aloneness, one is not alone: there is a depth which speaks to our depth; a spirit which meets with our spirit; an integrity which upholds us in our integrity; a love that does not give up on us even when we are tempted to give up on ourselves. Faith in God does not spare us from deep loneliness, but it puts that loneliness in a different light. He who can express his or her feelings in prayer is not alone. Prayer, in the midst of grief, is our personal affirmation that even though we are walking through the valley of the shadow of death we know that God is with us.

Turning Points. Grieving, like the healing of a wound, is a gradual process. There is no clear beginning and no clear ending; rather, there are stages along the way. But the journey of grief should lead to new feelings, new attitudes, fresh commitments, inner reorientations. If there is a time to be born and a time to die, there are also times to grieve and then to go beyond grieving. The "going beyond" grieving is a matter of steps or turning points. These turning points involve going beyond a pattern of withdrawal to a pattern of reaching out. They may involve such seemingly little things as rearranging some furniture, calling someone we have not talked to for a long time, going out somewhere, attending a movie or play or athletic contest, taking a class or a job. In taking the risk of reaching out one finds that there are resources to nurture us. Grief does not do its work automatically; our own inner willing and effort are required.

In discussing the spiritual meanings of suffering and grief Julius S. Bixler wrote, "We should remember, I think, that on whatever plane it comes religion is essentially devotion to that which as an intrinsic value frees us from slavery to our own petty purposes and from immersion in private grief." He recalls E. Stanley Jones' reference to Jesus' teaching that "we are to take up pain, calamity, injustice, and persecution, admit them into the purpose of our lives and make them contribute to higher ends—the ends for which we really live."[8] Out of the heart of grief there may come a deeper inwardness, a kindlier awareness of the needs of others, thoughts and feelings which lie too deep for words but which enrich the quality of our lives, a profounder sense of the reality and love of God, a heightened awareness of the wonder of life.

> I walked a mile with Pleasure.
>   She chattered all the way.
> But left me none the wiser
>   For all she had to say.
>
> I walked a mile with Sorrow.
>   And ne'er a word said she;
> But, oh, the things I learned from her
>   When Sorrow walked with me![9]

6. Making the Most of the Rest of Life:
Loneliness and Meaning in the Later Years

In this chapter we shall consider the later years—that span of life which includes the several years preceding retirement, the more active retirement years, and the years of declining strength and growing dependence on others. These are years which frequently bring loneliness. But we have good reason to believe that this is also a time which can bring new dimensions of meaning into our lives. Indeed, sometimes out of the experience of loneliness come important discoveries about oneself, about other persons, about life.

The Happy and Unhappy Sides of the Later Years

There is no escaping the fact that significant changes take place in us and around us in the later years. Life does not go on as usual. The person who is able to face these changes realistically and work out a style of life which is satisfying and productive is very fortunate.

The later years are likely to bring changes involving work, family, regularity of schedule, persons and places which have long been a part of our life, finances, status, health, and the world as we have known it. How we adjust to these changes and cope with the problems they bring profoundly influences what meaning life has for us in the later years.

Some of the problems of the later years are of a

very practical nature; they call for decisions regarding a place to live, finances, health care, and so forth. But there are other problems of critical importance which have to do with our attitudes, our feelings about ourselves and others, and our feelings about life. This is not surprising because the later years confront us with two crucial questions: *In relation to what do you find your identity? How do you find meaning in life?* These years are likely to bring changes which confront our sense of identity and personal worth. They also bring changes which challenge our concepts of what makes life meaningful. Without a sense of identity and personal worth, and without a sense of significance in living, human beings fall into deep, deep loneliness.

In our more active years our self-image and our satisfaction in living is related to roles we enact in work, family, and community. The later years bring changes in those roles. We do not always have the same sense of status, of being needed, of having something which needs to be done *now*.

"What I like least is the sharp reduction of social contacts . . . those associated with one's job."

"I do not like my present role as a spectator rather than participant . . . It is difficult to establish more than a superficial relation with new contemporaries."

"What proved most distressing was the ever present feeling of guilt which characterized those early weeks and months [of retirement]; the sense that I was wasting time and energy, that others were doing the work of the world all around me, and I alone was shirking."

"I found it hard to accept the situation of not being needed."

These quotations come from respondents to a survey conducted among a considerable number of retired persons for the Teachers Insurance and Annuity Association. Those who made the study have this to say about "the unhappy side of retirement": "Perhaps loneliness, loss of status, and lack of routine, coupled with boredom, are mentioned more often than other unpleasant circumstances." Added to these factors, of course, are problems related to inadequate finances and declining health.

If the later years have unhappy sides, they also have things on the plus side. Freedom from certain pressures, the chance to do things long postponed, the opportunity to enlarge one's world of experience with new interests, and the chance to render service through community groups and agencies are dimensions of the later years which can bring a sense of satisfaction and fulfillment.

Probably all persons who live into the later years have the experience of being looked upon and treated somewhat differently by those who are younger. To some it comes as something of a shock to realize that he or she is regarded as being "old" or "elderly" or "a senior citizen" by some around him. One of the tasks of the later years is that of fashioning a new self-image which is consistent with the facts, and achieving at least a measure of comfort with that new identity. Just as there is a time to be an infant, a child, an adolescent, a young adult, and a person of the middle years, so there is a time to experience the later years with dignity, meaning, and a measure of joy.

Needed in the Later Years:
A Mature Philosophy of Life

In Arthur Miller's play *Death of a Salesman* we meet an unforgettable figure, Willy Loman. Willy has a theory as to what life is all about. His aim in life is to be well-liked and to come out number one. Willy winds up a tragically lonely man. He does not come out number one. He is not known and appreciated and liked in the way he had wished. He cannot face up to being wrong about his own self-image and the axioms on which he has built his life. He cannot adjust to the fact that his old world has been swept away. His story is a tragic one because his answers to the questions of identity and meaning are so pathetically inadequate. His image of success and his philosophy of life fail him just when he most needs a mature view of what makes life significant.

One of the most important of all resources in our later years is a mature philosophy of life. Central to such a philosophy is the understanding that the purpose of life is to live and the purpose of being a human being is to be human and to grow in human qualities. Since being fully human involves creative relationships, success in living involves the quality of our relationships. The later years ought to represent a culmination in the art of living rather than the termination of a life of getting, winning, using, outdoing. Fortunate are those persons who carry into the later years a philosophy of life which treasures the values of heart and mind and spirit—and not simply the values of power, position, and possessions.

Although there are some values in life which can be achieved by aggressive methods and hard work, there are other values which are not achieved that way. These values come through sharing, appreciating, and giving and investing of oneself. Oscar Wilde once defined a cynic as "a man who knows the price of everything, and the value of nothing." There are some values which cannot be bought on the market at any price. They come only as we inwardly qualify for them. Someone said to an artist of one of his paintings, "I never saw a sunset which looked like that." To which the artist replied, "Don't you wish you could?"

Age can be measured chronologically, biologically, or psychologically. It is tragic if our philosophy misses the truth that the later years can have their own glory: accumulated wisdom, deep appreciation of the good and beautiful and true, a sense of wonder, integrity, the serenity which is born of a basic faith. The person who has nothing but years to prove his age is to be pitied.

In the earlier chapters of life we set goals for our living, we commit ourselves to certain values, and we adopt life-styles which reveal what we are really looking for in life. Hopefully those values, commitments, and life-styles help prepare us for the later years. If not, we are likely to feel estranged from life and meaning as we grow older. But it is never too late to become wiser about the deeper meanings of life. For some, the most creative adventure of the later years is essentially spiritual in character—as we seek and act out a more mature philosophy of what life is really all about.

The Later Years: A Time for Simplifying

During young adulthood and the middle years we are likely to be very busy, hurried, beset with more things to do than we know how to handle. How frequently life is likened to a rat race! One of the advantages of the later years is the opportunity to enjoy a less pressured kind of existence. But to enjoy that existence one must practice the art of simplifying life.

In *Walden* Henry Thoreau had some interesting things to say on this subject. "Our life is frittered away by detail . . . . Simplify, simplify . . . . I love a broad margin to my life." Some years ago Lewis Sherrill wrote a helpful book *The Struggle Of The Soul*. He expressed the conviction that the central need of the later years is that of "achieving simplification of life in its physical, material and spiritual aspects, so that the soul may with less and less impediment progress toward its chosen destiny." The destiny we choose has to do with what we want our lives to mean. Simplification involves focusing on what we really think is most important, and pushing into the margin those things which are irrelevant. I have some friends who greet guests who come to their simply-furnished mountain cabin with the words, "If you need something we don't have, tell us—and we'll explain how you can get along without it." It is amazing how much satisfying living can be done without benefit of many of the *things* and *activities* and *appointments* and *preoccupations* which have so greatly concerned us in earlier years.

The best way to simplify life will vary from person to person. It is likely, however, to involve having some plans for each day but with fewer demands, having some provision for bodily exercise without trying to function as though we were ten or twenty years younger than we are, appreciating material things we have around us without forever accumulating more things to fill our lives. A couple who recently moved into a retirement home where they have much less room than they had in their rather sizeable house commented, "We are discovering that for years we have been carrying things around with us that did no earthly good." How wonderful it would be if we could learn earlier in life what things are really important in the life we regard as significant.

The problem of loneliness in the later years cannot be solved by trying to go on as usual or by trying to fill our lives with more things. One road to the alleviation of loneliness is in the simplification of life to the end that we can focus on those relationships and appreciations and dimensions of the inner life which give life meaning.

As he came to the later years of his life Dr. Albert Schweitzer wrote these words:

> My hair is beginning to turn. My body is beginning to show traces of the exertions I have demanded of it, and of the passage of the years.
>
> I look back with thankfulness to the time when, without needing to husband my strength, I could get through an uninterrupted course of bodily and mental work. With calmness and humility I look forward to the future, so that I may not be unprepared for renunciation if it is required of me. Whether we be workers or sufferers, it is assuredly our duty to conserve our powers, as being men who have won their way through to the peace which passeth all understanding.[1]

The Later Years: A Time for Taking In

Just as our physical bodies require proper food and diet, so our minds and spirits require adequate nourishment. We need balanced diets for the whole person. A publication of the American Medical Association says, "Total health involves the spiritual, the emotional and the social aspects of life as well as the physical." In the later years it is important that attention be given to the nourishment of our total selves. Without proper nourishment we more easily fall victim to discouragement, boredom, and loneliness.

Our minds need continuing nourishment and challenge. Studies indicate that the capacity for learning continues into the later years. Education can be lifelong. One of the surest ways to combat loneliness is to keep one's curiosity alive. Herman Laff, a Denver physician, retired from his practice at the age of sixty-seven. He long had interests in religion but had not made any kind of systematic study of the subject. He began taking courses in the Iliff School of Theology on a noncredit basis. Over a period of years he took enough courses that he would have been eligible for graduation had he been taking them for credit. The school made him an honorary alumnus! In the meantime he contributed richly to the school community by his presence there. Gabriel Mason, who has passed his ninetieth birthday, has written of the importance of keeping mentally alive through habits of asking questions and learning. In an article for the *NRTA Journal* he stated: "It is easy to sit back and daydream or to take a place in the corner by the fireside and gaze into empty space. This, however, is self-destructive. Life at all ages is meant to be lived actively, spiced with curiosity, inquisitiveness and the love of learning." Reading, discussion groups, and classes are among the ways in which we may meet our needs for mental intake.

Likewise, we need food for our emotions through human associations; through the experience of beauty in nature, in growing things, in music, and other forms of art; through worship. It has been said that some persons yearn for endless life who don't know what to do with a rainy afternoon. Through the feeding of the inner life we are saved from inner emptiness of spirit. In Denver we have a radio announcer, Gene Amole, who loves to comment on things happening in the world of nature. He has a microphone just outside the window; he gives his listeners a running account of how the birds are doing. He calls attention to things of beauty close at hand. Early one morning recently he called attention to an especially beautiful sunrise. "Get up," he said, "and see it. No one can keep it from you except yourself!"

Spiritual health also requires that we keep alive our sense of wonder and our sense of the mysterious. G. K. Chesterton said, "The world will never starve for lack of wonders, but only for lack of wonder." Albert Einstein wrote:

> The most beautiful thing we can experience is the mysterious. It is the source of all true art and science. He to whom this emotion is a stranger, who can no longer pause to wonder and stand rapt in awe, is as good as dead: his eyes are closed . . . . To know that what is impenetrable to us really exists, manifesting itself as the highest wisdom and the most radiant beauty which our dull faculties can comprehend only in their most primitive forms—this knowledge, this feeling is at the center of true religiousness.[2]

The later years, like all other years, are for taking in those sources of renewal which make for wholeness.

The Later Years: A Time for Sharing and Contributing

A Mother Superior who chose to remain anonymous wrote this prayer:

Lord, Thou knowest better than I know myself that I am growing older, and will some day be old.

Keep me from getting talkative, and particularly from the fatal habit of thinking I must say something on every subject and on every occasion.

Release me from craving to try to straighten out everybody's affairs.

Keep my mind free from the recital of endless details—give me wings to get to the point.

I ask for grace enough to listen to the tales of others' pains. Help me to endure them with patience.

But seal my lips on my own aches and pains—they are increasing and my love of rehearsing them is becoming sweeter as the years go by.

Teach me the glorious lesson that occasionally it is possible that I may be mistaken.

Keep me reasonably sweet; I do not want to be a saint—some of them are so hard to live with—but a sour old woman is one of the crowning works of the devil.

Make me thoughtful, but not moody; helpful, but not bossy. With my vast store of wisdom, it seems a pity not to use it all—but Thou knowest, Lord, that I want a few friends at the end.[3]

The wise author of these words knew that one of the hazards of the later years is that of becoming overly preoccupied with oneself. The best remedy for that is a healthy interest in others and the readiness to do some sharing and contributing.

When in his seventies John R. Voris wrote an article entitled "Let Senior Citizens Serve Others!" He wrote:

If one were to judge by some of the popular presentations of the problems of aging, he would conclude that the sole goal of life is to live to a comfortable old age. To what end, I would ask; where lies the virtue in just getting old? All the benefits being provided for senior citizens—golden years clubs, bus rides, picnics, crafts classes, good housing, better health, retirement homes—are good in themselves. But what is the use of them unless a person can pursue a purpose beyond oneself? It is here that the problem of old age assumes moral, psychological and spiritual aspects fully as important as physical well-being.[4]

He went on to suggest ways in which older persons can share their experience and abilities through community groups, volunteer agencies, and person-to-person relationships.

Older persons vary in their capacities for serving and contributing; health factors and other considerations enter in. But surely the point is an important one—one of the surest roads to inner satisfaction is in being of use to someone else. We all need to be needed. Loneliness is the inevitable result of feeling that we are not needed, that we mean nothing to anyone else. Too often we carry with us the image of the later years as a time for being "put on the shelf" or "sidelined." It need not always be so.

It is a rare day in which we cannot speak the encouraging word to someone, write a note, or make a call to someone in need. Many in their later years are able to do more active things through groups and agencies of various kinds. There are resources through churches and social agencies to help us discover where some of the needs are.

The Later Years: A Time for Being

Some older persons contribute richly to the world simply by being who and what they are.

Hazel Kerr looked with joy upon a child, then a youth, and finally upon one who had lived many years—years which had brought an inner quality of life which only years of living can bring. There she saw a pair of tranquil eyes. Deep within them burned a steady light of understanding that youth has never known—"the light of understanding and of grace, that quiet strength that comes when souls have grown full statured."

Our culture is so oriented toward work and activity that we often fail to recognize the contribution of older persons who serve the world by being who and what they are. The New Testament says, "Let no one despise your youth" (I Timothy 4:12). The same might be said of each chapter of life including the later years. In the cycle of life the later years have their distinctive place and meanings.

The world needs living examples of the wisdom which can come only out of experience—the wisdom which affirms the road which has been travelled, even as it affirms the road ahead, and the next generation.

The world needs living examples of the serenity which comes from having outlived many things, from having made one's mental peace with the fundamental ways of things, from a deep-rooted faith. Robert Browning pictures the aged rabbi who has survived so much saying, "The future I may face, now I have proved the past."

The world needs living examples of personal pride and self-esteem under adverse circumstances. Recently the newspapers carried a story telling of a contest held among women residents of Illinois nursing homes. One of the residents, Elizabeth Barrett, aged ninety, was named "Ms. Nursing Home Of Illinois." On winning she said, "I believe in helping those who need help." To be who we are and where we are with a sense of wholesome self-esteem and interest in others is an important way of serving the world—and minimizing loneliness.

The world also needs living examples of older persons who keep affirming life in varied ways and who encourage others simply by their appreciations of what life brings. My friend and barber, Elmer Wells, is well into his eighties. His shop, across the street from the University of Denver campus, is a special place—because Elmer is there. He frequently expresses what he is feeling in poetry. Some time ago he wrote:

Some years from now when you are tired
　Of all life's troubles, grief and care
You take a stroll into the woods
　In hope to find some solace there.
On each flower in the woods you see
　The planet of sweet memory.
On every bush and plant you find
　Dear dreams of friends you left behind.

The song birds in the trees will bring
　The voice of loved ones as they sing.
The silent gentle flowing brook
　Gives you kind faces as you look.
You rest beneath a lovely tree
　You are relaxed and feel so free.
You sit as silent as a stone
　You feel so great, yet all alone.

And as the evening shadows fall
　You feel so blessed that after all
The lessons nature gave were true
　Beauty is seen in every view.
A silent voice speaks in your ear
　You're not alone, someone is here.
You breathe a deep refreshing sigh
　God brought you here, He's standing by.

Finally, the world needs living examples of a faith that looks to the future with courage and hope. Justice Oliver Wendell Holmes expressed that courage and hope in these words written in his later years:

As I grow older I grow calm. If I feel what are perhaps an old man's apprehensions . . . if I fear that we are running through the world's resources at a pace that we cannot keep, I do not lose my hopes. I do not pin my dreams for the future to my country or even to my race. I think it probable that civilization will last as long as I care to look ahead—perhaps with smaller numbers, but perhaps also bred to greatness and splendor by science. I think it not improbable that man, like the grub that prepares a chamber for the winged thing it never has seen but is to be—that man may have cosmic destinies that he does not understand. And so beyond the vision of battling races and an impoverished earth I catch a dreaming glimpse of peace.

The other day my dream was pictured to my mind. I was walking homeward on Pennsylvania Avenue . . . as I looked beyond Sherman's statue to the west the city was aflame with scarlet and crimson from the setting sun . . . . But, below the skyline there came from little globes the pallid discord of the electric lights. And I thought to myself . . . from those globes clustered like evil eggs will come the new masters of the sky. It is like the time in which we live. But then I remembered the faith that I partly have expressed, faith in a universe not measured by our fears, a universe that has thought and more than thought inside of it, and as I gazed, after the sunset, and above the electric lights, there shone the stars.[5]

Loneliness is very real in the later years. But so are faith and hope and love.

Part Three

RESOURCES AND STRATEGIES FOR DEALING WITH LONELINESS

Let your soul speak for itself. Some souls hold conversation with God in music, and some in the sowing of seed, and others in the smell of sawed wood, and still others in the affectionate understanding of their friends. All souls are not alike. Utter your own prayer, in the language of your own joy. Repent of your own sin and let your lament be your own sorrow and not another's. When you worship, thank God for whatever has given you joy, though it be so slight that no other soul would think it worthy of mention. Let your own insights sing their praise of creation, and your own handiwork adore the Invisible Creator.

Quit dressing your soul in somebody else's piety. Your soul is not a pauper. Let it live its own life. Truth is just as necessary for the life of the soul as faith and humility, and truth is not merely the final and authoritative statement of the universe's wide design or life's deepest meaning—no, truth is the soul being itself.

If then you have begun to build, remember that beginning is not enough. Take upon yourself the disciplines of growth; live freely and in faith; keep your eyes alert and your soul humble that you may not miss the visit of the eternal in your neighborhood of circumstance and experience. Most of all, untie your soul, give it room to breathe, let it play, do not be ashamed of it. It is the child of the eternal and destined for greater things than you know.

Samuel H. Miller

7. Out of Loneliness—New Life

In the preceding chapters we have considered several forms of loneliness. We have reckoned with the deep pain of loneliness in various seasons and experiences of life. We come now to the question: What does the experience of loneliness come to mean to us? What does it do to us and in us? Can any good possibly come out of it?

In this chapter we shall develop the position that there are three major resources for dealing with loneliness: (1) *an inner life* of positive interests and appreciations and a sense of humor, (2) *a religious faith* which helps us to see life in its wholeness, which helps us find purpose and meaning in our lives, and which undergirds us with the assurance of God's presence in all times and places, (3) *a renewing life-style* of keeping in touch with the world about us, with events, with our own selves, and with what might be.

In this chapter we shall also see that the experience of loneliness can make a positive contribution to our lives if out of it there comes the search for a richer inner life, a deeper religious faith, and a more creative life-style. The experience of loneliness is not something to be sought, but in its coming it can make a positive contribution to our lives, if we will it to be so. If loneliness is the feeling of not being meaningfully related, it is good news to know that there are some things which can be done to enter into deeper relations with self, with other persons, with events, and with God, bringing newness of life.

The Inner Life

The mind is its own place,
and in itself
Can make a heaven of hell, a hell of heaven.

In these words John Milton pointed to the importance of one's inner life. We cannot always change external facts, but we can do something about our responses to them. We can also have an inner life of meaning even in the midst of adverse circumstances. Some of our loneliness is related to external facts which we cannot change; but often we can do something about the life we live in our minds. We are not fated to be the victims of self-pity, inner emptiness of spirit, boredom.

Being Interested. William Lyon Phelps said, "The happiest person is he who thinks the most interesting thoughts." At least, a person who has interesting thoughts will not be bored—and boredom is the most deadly thing in the world.

The experience of loneliness forces us to confront ourselves. If we are prepared to listen to its message loneliness tells us that in some important respects we must take responsibility for our own lives. There are some things no one else is going to do for us. It is easy enough to withdraw within ourselves and focus our attention upon ourselves. Some of that is needed, but if shutting out the persons and events around us becomes a way of life we are in deep trouble. The fact of the matter is that there *are* interesting events and ideas and persons to which we can give some attention. What gets your attention gets you.

Paul Tillich once said, "Loneliness can be conquered only by those who can bear solitude." If we cannot bear solitude, if we must always be in a crowd or with other persons, we probably will know much of loneliness. But one need not be lonely in times of solitude if he has an inner life of positive interests. This is what Louisa Alcott meant about her own solitude in prolonged illness when she said, "I enjoyed my mind." Solitude can actually be creative. Indeed, few creative things have been done in science, in art, or in living without times of solitude. The greatest religious leaders have required times of solitude.

A distinguished educator once said, "The purpose of education is to produce curious people"—by which, of course, he meant persons with curiosity. As long as one is curious about what has gone on in the world and what is continuing to happen in it, about ideas, about persons, he or she will be less lonely. No day in which we have learned something that we did not know before is a lost day or a completely lonely day. As long as we find life interesting we are alive—even though our life may not be easy. It is possible to participate mentally in the world about us even in solitude. Zona Gale pointed to a central truth about keeping inwardly alive when she said that the first article in her creed was "I believe in expanding the areas of my awareness." To be aware is to be less lonely.

Our Appreciations. In a memorable article entitled "Three Days To See" Hellen Keller listed the things she would most wish to see if by some miracle she might be granted three days of sight. Most of the things she listed are available to most of us every day. She concluded her article with these words:

I who am blind can give one hint to those who see: Use your eyes as if tomorrow you would be stricken blind. And the same can be applied to the other senses.

Hear the music of voices, the song of a bird, the mighty strains of an orchestra as if you would be stricken deaf tomorrow. Touch each object as if tomorrow your tactile sense would fail. Smell the perfume of flowers, taste with relish each morsel, as if tomorrow you could never smell or taste again. Make the most of every sense; glory in all the facets of pleasure and beauty which the world reveals to you through the several means of contact which nature provides. But of all the senses, I am sure that sight must be far and away the most delightful.[1]

In these words Helen Keller reminds us that around us is a world of wonder, beauty, growth, and meaning; but we must be open to it if it is to become a part of our inner lives. That person is rich whose inner life is fed by good music, interesting reading, hobbies, a sense of companionship with the good and the great of all times. He has inner resources which save him from the need of constantly being entertained or continually having people around him.

Toward the end of his life Charles Darwin said:

If I had my life to live again, I would have made a rule to read some poetry and listen to some music at least once every week; for perhaps the parts of my brain now atrophied would thus have been kept alive through use. The loss of these tastes is a loss of happiness, and may possibly be injurious to the intellect, and more probably to the moral character, by enfeebling the emotional part of our nature.

An essential ingredient in a rich inner life is a sense of wonder. William Davies said, "A poor life this, if full of care, we have no time to stand and stare." Emerson said that if the stars were to appear only one night in a thousand years persons would speak for generations of the wondrous sight which had been seen. How much we take for granted! Let no

day pass without appreciating something or someone, or simply saying "How wonderful!"

A Sense of Humor. A tablet in Chester Cathedral,
England, carries this poem written by an anonymous author:

> Give me a good digestion, Lord,
> And also something to digest.
> Give me a healthy body, Lord,
> With sense to keep it at its best.

> Give me a healthy mind, Lord,
> To keep the good and pure in sight,
> Which, seeing sin, is not appalled
> But finds a way to set it right.

> Give me a mind that is not bored,
> That does not whimper, whine or sigh;
> Don't let me worry overmuch
> About the fussy thing called I.

> Give me a sense of humor, Lord,
> Give me the grace to see a joke,
> To get some happiness from life
> And pass it on to other folk.

Viktor Frankl has told how in the loneliness and
agony of Nazi concentration camps a sense of
humor was a saving thing for some of the prisoners.
Centuries ago it was said, "A cheerful heart is a
good medicine, but a downcast spirit dries up the
bones" (Proverbs 17:22). In 1950 Bennett Cerf
wrote:

Never in history has the average American citizen found more
need for a saving sense of humor. Beset by threats of destruction
by atomic bombs, inflation, mounting taxes, overcrowded cities,
witch hunters, propagandists, caterwauling commentators, and
the incessant clamor of radio and television commercials, he
must laugh occasionally to keep from blowing his top altogether.
It's far too easy today to see only the shadows, and ignore the
patches of sunlight that remain.[2]

If these words were relevant in 1950, how much more so are they today! Humor always has an important place in life. There are many problems—including loneliness—which it does not solve. But it helps to lift us out of ourselves and to put things in truer perspective. As we think of the resources for dealing with loneliness a wholesome sense of humor needs to be taken into account. The metrical Scotch version of the One Hundredth Psalm calls us to unite the spirit of worship with the spirit of good humor:

> All people that on earth do dwell
> Sing to the Lord with cheerful voice,
> Him serve with mirth, His praise forth tell
> Come ye before Him and rejoice!

Religious Faith and the Life of Devotion

To the question "Which commandment is the first of all?" Jesus answered:

The first is, "Hear, O Israel: The Lord our God, the Lord is one; and you shall love the Lord your God with all your heart, and with all your soul, and with all your mind, and with all your strength."

The second is this, "You shall love your neighbor as yourself." There is no other commandment greater than these.

(Mark 12:29-31)

These are familiar words. But what is it to love God with heart, soul, strength, and mind? It is more than obeying a set of rules or having certain feelings or belonging to a particular church or synagogue. It involves a total way of life. It includes a way of seeing life, of getting things put together, of choosing values and making commitments. Anyone who is serious about wanting to love God with heart, soul, strength, and mind is trying to face up to what life is all about. He is saying that life can be more than a rat race, a meaningless routine, a matter of consuming things and then leaving behind an empty dish. He is affirming that life can have depth and purpose and meaning in response to the Source and Sustainer of life—God.

Some years ago Arnold Toynbee raised the question as to whether there is progress in history. Speaking out of his Christian heritage, he said:

> If man has been created in the likeness of God, and if the true end of man is to make this likeness ever more and more like, then Aristotle's saying that "man is a social animal" applies to man's highest potentiality and aim—that of trying to get into ever closer communion with God. Seeking God is itself a social act.
> He [the Christian] is a citizen of the Kingdom of God, and therefore his paramount and all-embracing aim is to attain the highest degree of communion with and likeness to God Himself; . . . his way of loving his neighbour as himself will be to try to help his neighbour to win what he is seeking for himself—that is, to come into closer communion with God and to become more godlike.
> The matter in which there might be spiritual progress in time on a time-span extending over many successive generations of life on Earth is . . . the opportunity open to souls, by way of the learning that comes through suffering, for getting into closer communion with God, and becoming less unlike Him, during their passage through this world.[3]

These are indeed serious words coming from one who has long reflected on the human situation. Toynbee is saying that there can be a God-oriented life, that a person's chief concern can be that of living in communion with God and becoming more Godlike. His words reflect what Jesus said centuries ago.

But is this a realistic teaching as we look at the actual world? We see so many persons organizing life around themselves and their desire for power, position, possessions, self-indulgent pleasure. Is it realistic to suppose that ordinary persons can ever seek another kind of life?

H. Richard Niebuhr often said that human beings organize their lives around "centers of value." Differences in life-styles can often be traced back to differences in centers of value. We place our trust and devotion in different things. At the heart of great religion is the conviction that beyond our many lesser gods is the Ultimate-Real-Other with whom we have to deal in life and death. Religion affirms that there *is* a quality of life really worth the living, and that life is one in which we seek to organize our living around the Ultimate-Real-Other we call God.

Many attempts have been made to speak of God. All reveal the inadequacy of human language. But in the struggle to affirm that which can never be fully expressed, something important is being communicated. We are not alone. In life and death we are profoundly related. This is what great religion is all about. Its marks are trust and devotion and love.

Religion is a matter of believing, but it is more. It is a matter of acting, but it is more. It is a matter of contact and communion with that which is central and enduring in the nature of things. Spirit with Spirit meets.

In *Mixed Pasture* Evelyn Underhill spoke of "that mysterious Something Other, the Holy, which gives meaning to life."

H. Richard Niebuhr wrote, "This reality . . . is something with which we must all reckon . . . the secret of existence by virtue of which things come into being, are what they are, and pass away.

Against it there is no defense. This reality abides when all else passes ... insofar as our faith, our reliance for meaning and worth has been attached to this source and enemy of all our gods, we have been enabled to call this reality God."

William Ernest Hocking spoke of "the presence of an actual Thou-art ... It is there."

Six centuries before Christ, Lao-tzu, a Chinese philosopher, said, "As rivers have their source in some far-off fountain, so the human spirit has its source. To find this fountain of spirit is to learn the secret of heaven and earth."

The French philosopher Émile Boutroux spoke simply of "the Beyond that is within."

Alan Watts has written, "For creativity and sanity man needs to have, or at least to feel, a meaningful relation to and union with life, with reality itself .... Without this man cannot feel that his life has any actual and objective meaning."

At the heart of Jesus' message were the words, "Seek first his kingdom and his righteousness, and all these things shall be yours as well" (Matthew 6:33).

Words such as these sound strange to many in today's activity-oriented, success-oriented, consuming-oriented culture. But they communicate a wisdom which is our ultimate defense against emptiness of spirit and loneliness.

Prayer, worship, communion, and meditation are among the human responses to "the Beyond that is within." He who so responds—not in order to use God, but to draw closer to God and to become more Godlike—knows in the depths of his being that he is not ultimately alone.

Reference was made in an earlier chapter to

Alfred North Whitehead's teaching that religion begins with a sense of solitariness. It moves through various stages, culminating in the experience of God the companion. It was Whitehead who also called attention to the interrelated themes of permanence and change in great religion. The hymn expresses these themes in the familiar words

> Abide with me:
> fast falls the eventide.

If out of the experience of loneliness there comes the sincere search for deeper religious understanding and experience, loneliness will have served us well. Where there is trust in and devotion to the One who abides, there is faith and hope and love.

A Life-Style of Keeping in Touch

The experience of loneliness comes to all persons. What that experience does to us and in us, how we cope with it, and how we incorporate it into our ongoing experience depends in part on our life-style. If our life-style is basically one of avoiding relationships and is one of withdrawal, loneliness will pose a very special problem. If our life-style involves an openness to relationships, we will have more resources with which to cope with it. There is also a greater chance that something creative will come out of the pain of loneliness.

Three important factors are involved in a truly satisfying and fulfilling life-style: (1) exercising our creative powers, (2) living one day at a time, and (3) keeping in touch with the sources of renewal.

Exercising Our Creative Powers. Loneliness is intensified when we think of ourselves as being completely at the mercy of external circumstances. But it is a rare situation in which we cannot do something which will help create a better attitude or situation. Human beings do not merely *react* to external circumstances; they have the power to *respond* with something creative of their own. Trouble may color life, but we have a voice in determining what the color is going to be.

Erich Fromm reminds us that we all have two opposing wishes at the same time—one is to regress and the other is to reach out and grow. In exercising the will to grow we experience the joy of creation. He puts it this way:

Man is always torn between the wish to regress and the wish to be fully born. Every act of birth requires the courage to let go of something, to let go of the womb, to let go of the breast, to let go of the lap, to let go of the hand, to let go eventually of all certainties, and to rely only upon one thing: one's own powers to be aware and to respond; that is, one's own creativity. To be creative is to consider the whole process of life as a process of birth, and not to take any stage of life as a final stage. Most people die before they are fully born. Creativeness means to be born before one dies . . . .

Without courage and faith, creativity is impossible, and hence the understanding and cultivation of courage and faith are indispensable conditions for the development of the creative attitude.

Let me say again that creativity in this sense does not refer to a quality which particularly gifted persons or artists could achieve, but to an attitude which every human being should and can achieve. Education for creativity is nothing short of education for living.[4]

These are encouraging words. They help us to believe that life can be an art and that each of us can share in the processes of creation in his situation. We can share in creating our own life—a meaningful life—within the limits we cannot escape. Life is the art of the possible. We all share in creating the world of our experience, in creating a psychological environment, in creating relationships.

A friend said, "I hope I can keep on planting seeds as long as I live." He will never feel completely victimized by external circumstance. He knows that he has it in him to share in the creation of the world.

Nicholas Johnson, a busy administrator, has written about what he is trying to do in creating a more meaningful life for himself. He thinks that most of us are too dependent on what other people do for us, on what we can buy ready-made, on things that can be consumed. He advocates a way of life in which persons share in the creating of their own play and entertainment, in their own mental growth, in their reaching out to persons and groups and experiences which makes one more alive. In this process he finds that the writing of a daily journal is immensely helpful in nurturing one's sense of sharing in the creation of one's own life. He writes:

> I find that all the elements of life I have described are served by writing in my journal . . . it's not a diary. It's a sketchbook, a workbook for life. Its poems, recipes, love notes, furniture designs, speech drafts, silly thoughts, serious reflections, and drawings, all mixed together, as life is—or should be. It's a tangible record of the balance in your life. It makes you see better, take life with more seriousness and more whimsey. I like it.[5]

The creative person sustains expectations of what life can be. He recognizes that as the years pass we as persons are likely to flatten out or flower out. The road to new births and continuing growth is in day-by-day decisions as we respond to events in mature and creative ways. Edna St. Vincent Millay writes of a love that passed, when it did not need to:

> 'Tis not love's going hurts my days
> But that it went in little ways.[6]

We ourselves create so much of the meaning or loss
of meaning in our lives—day by day, in little ways
and in ordinary events.

Living One Day At a Time.

> Look to this day!
> For it is life, the very life of life.
> In its brief course lie all the verities
>   and realities of your existence:
> The bliss of growth;
> The glory of action;
> The splendor of beauty;
> For yesterday is already a dream, and
>   tomorrow is only a vision;
> But today, well lived, makes every yesterday
> A Dream of happiness, and every tomorrow
>   a vision of hope.
> Look well, therefore, to this day.
> Such is the salutation of the dawn!
>   (from the Sanskrit)

Every experience of loneliness is experienced in
some particular day. Every experience of meaning,
and victory over loneliness, is experienced in some
particular day. He who would cope with loneliness
must learn the fine art of living one day at a time,
seeking whatever meanings that day might afford.
In each day we need to be open to meaning, open to
beauty, open to love, open to God, open to joy.

Life is given us one day at a time. Each day can
be a life in miniature. The glory of a life well lived is
the glory of single days well lived. Those values of
heart and mind and spirit which we would most like
to characterize our lives, can be sought and found
and expressed in each today.

If we are passing through a time of difficulty, we should let each day be sufficient unto itself. Today will provide strength for itself, and tomorrow will bring strength for tomorrow's needs. Someone has written, "Life is hard by the yard; by the inch it's a cinch." That may be oversimplifying things, but there is truth in the statement. If we can muster the courage for the living of this day, tomorrow will bring resources.

If today we are relatively sound of mind and body, and if things are going reasonably well, then we can let this very day be a day for coming alive to the goodness and beauty and wonder about us and affirming our part in the mystery and wonder of creation. We can let this be the day for feeling and celebrating our unity with the whole of which we are a part. This can be a day for caring and sharing and being reborn. "This is the day which the LORD has made; let us rejoice and be glad in it" (Psalm 118:24).

Martin Buber wrote, "God speaks to every man through the life He gives him again and again. Therefore man can only answer God with the whole of life—with the way in which he lives this given life . . . There is no true human share of holiness without the hallowing of the everyday." He who approaches each day with the sense that life is a gift to be hallowed, will not be spared the experience of loneliness, but his loneliness will not be without meaning.

Keeping in Touch with the Sources of Renewal. Our life-style, our way of life, expresses how we are getting things put together. It reveals our self-image, the values we are seeking and finding, our commitments. Many things go into a life-style: how and what a person eats, his sleeping habits, what he wears, the language he uses, the songs he sings and the music he listens to, the arrangements he makes for human relating, his expectations of life, his methods in decision-making, his feelings about past, present, and future, his perceptions of and responses to the pivotal experiences of life including work, play, love, suffering, aging, death. A life-style includes the way one organizes his time, and expends his energies. A life-style is one's way of being in the world. It is one's way of saying, "Here I am."

A person can think of himself or herself as being basically a cog in a machine, a rat in a rat race, a commodity in the marketplace of business, a consumer of goods. There are life-styles which reflect these various self-images. The tragic fact is that every one of these life-styles tends to separate the person from his own human self, and from other persons as human beings. Persons are treated, not as human beings, but as things, objects, commodities. The inevitable result of such life-styles is deep loneliness of spirit. There is much feeling of emptiness and unfulfillment in our world due to inadequate images of what it is to be a person. There is profound loneliness attached to making a career of enacting less-than-human roles.

The purpose of life is to live. The purpose of being a human being is to become more fully human. These goals are never completely realized, but we can move toward them every day of our lives. What is needed are self-renewing life-styles wherein the individual is in touch with himself, with the world of nature about him, with other persons, with creative activity, and with causes and purposes beyond his own self-interest. Such life-styles not only provide a defense against the inroads of loneliness, they bring a sense of inner fulfillment and a lasting contribution to the world.

It was over sixty years ago that Richard Cabot wrote his book *What Men Live By*. Dr. Cabot identified four great sources of renewal and meaning: work, play, love, and worship. Many years later, a physician who had studied with Dr. Cabot in the Harvard Medical School, said that this little book summed up much of the wisdom about health of spirit which he had learned through his psychiatric experience. He suggested that we think of life as a table with four legs in balance—work, play, love, and worship. He then suggested putting a vase of flowers on the table to represent this very day, incorporating into each day something of work and play and love and worship. Surely this is a very good start on a renewing and fulfilling life-style. Any person who follows this life-style will feel inwardly alive as a human being.

Life comes to mean such different things to different persons. How wonderful it is when we meet a human being who is warmly, happily, lovingly alive. Such a person lights our candle, renews our spirit, and encourages us to live the day with greater courage, hope, and joy. Such a person is not wholly preoccupied with self, but has found a way of uniting a healthy self-interest with an interest in other persons and in causes which are worthy of one's self-investment. William James said that the great use of a life is to spend it for something which will outlast it.

The experience of loneliness goes very deep. There is no way of escaping it. But it often can be turned to constructive ends if we wish it to be so. If out of it we are led to move toward a deeper and richer inner life—including a greater degree of self-understanding, if we are turned toward a deeper religious faith, and if we learn something about what makes life significant, then loneliness will have served us in very important ways.

It has been said that pain conquered is power. So we might say, loneliness dealt with creatively yields power. What is even more important, it yields wisdom and a deeper understanding of what it is to be a human being.

When John Greenleaf Whittier was seventy-one years of age he wrote a poem entitled "At Eventide." It reflects a life well-lived, a life which had known both loneliness and rich associations, a life lived in touch with the realities which give life meaning.

> Yet, not unthankfully,
> I call to mind the fountains by the way,
> The breath of flowers, the bird-song on the spray,
> Dear friends, sweet human loves, the joy of giving
> And of receiving, the great boon of living
> In grand historic years when Liberty
> Had need of word and work, quick sympathies
> For all who fail and suffer, song's relief,
> Nature's uncloying loveliness; and chief,
> The kind restraining hand of Providence,
> The inward witness, the assuring sense
> Of an Eternal Good which overlies
> The sorrow of the world, Love which outlives
> All sin and wrong, Compassion which forgives
> To the uttermost, and Justice whose clear eyes
> Through lapse and failure look to the intent,
> And judge our frailty by the life we meant.

NOTES

Chapter One

1. Robert Frost, "Revelation," *The Poetry of Robert Frost* (New York: Holt, Rinehart and Winston, 1969), p. 19.
2. Erich Fromm, *The Art of Loving* (New York: Bantam Books, 1967), pp. 82, 72, 73.
3. Erich Fromm, *The Revolution of Hope* (New York: Bantam Books, 1968), p. 1.
4. A. N. Whitehead, *Religion in the Making* (New York: Macmillan Co., 1926), pp. 16, 17, 19, 20, 60.
5. Gordon Allport, *The Individual and His Religion* (New York: Macmillan Co., 1950), p. 142.
6. John Gardner, *Self-Renewal* (New York: Harper & Row, 1965), p. 102.
7. Viktor Frankl, *Man's Search for Meaning* (New York: Washington Square Press, 1963), pp. 213, 122.

Chapter Two

1. René A. Spitz, "Life and the Dialogue," in *Counterpoint* (New York: International Universities Press, 1963), p. 174.
2. David Elkind, *Erik H. Erikson: Psychosocial Analyst* (Nutley, N.J.: Roche Laboratories, nd), p. 7.
3. Theodore Lidz, *The Person* (New York: Basic Books, 1968), pp. 298-99.
4. Erik Erikson, "Identity and the Life Cycle," in *Psychological Issues* (New York: International Universities Press, 1959), p. 98.
5. Olga Knopf, "Grow Old and Enjoy It," *NRTA Journal*, 26 (September-October 1975), p. 9.
6. H. E. Fosdick, *The Living of These Days* (New York: Harper & Brothers, 1956), pp. 312, 319.

Chapter Three

1. W. H. Auden, "New Year Letter," *The Collected Poetry of W. H. Auden* (New York: Random House, 1945), p. 311.
2. Eugene O'Neill, *Long Day's Journey Into Night* (New Haven: Yale University Press, 1956), pp. 153-54.

3. Carl Sandburg, "Fish Crier," *The Complete Poems of Carl Sandburg* (New York: Harcourt Brace Jovanovich, 1970), p. 10.

Chapter Four

1. Ina May Greer, "Roots of Loneliness," *Pastoral Psychology*, 4 (June 1953), p. 28.
2. Bill Adler, comp., *The Wisdom of Martin Luther King* (New York: Lancer Books, 1968), p. 114.
3. W. E. Hocking, *The Coming World Civilization* (New York: Harper & Brothers, 1956), p. 186.
4. E. Mansell Pattison, "The Experience of Dying," *American Journal of Psychotherapy*, 21 (January 1967), pp. 32-43.
5. Carl Nighswonger, "Some Christian Perspectives on Death and Dying," *Together*, 15 (June 1971), p. 11.
6. Stewart Alsop, *Stay of Execution: A Sort of Memoir* (Philadelphia: J. B. Lippincott Co., 1973), p. 11.
7. Pierre Teilhard de Chardin, *Hymn of the Universe* (New York: Harper & Row, 1965), pp. 103-04.

Chapter Five

1. Ralph Cokain, "A Loneliness I Never Expected," *New York Times* (March 24, 1972).
2. Colin Parkes, *Bereavement* (New York: International Universities Press, 1972), pp. 164-65.
3. *Ibid.*, p. 118.
4. Quoted by Joshua Liebman in *Current Religious Thought* (April 1947), p. 6.
5. Helen Hayes, "In My Darkest Hour—Hope," in *A Treasury of Comfort*, ed. Sidney Greenberg (New York: Crown Publishers, 1954), p. 164.
6. John Gunther, *Death Be Not Proud* (New York: Modern Library 1953), pp. 190-91.
7. *Ibid.*, pp. 259-60.
8. J. S. Bixler, *Education for Adversity* (Cambridge: Harvard University Press, 1952), pp. 22-23.
9. Robert Browning Hamilton, "Along the Road," *Treasury of Comfort*, p. 219.

Chapter Six

1. Albert Schweitzer, *Out of My Life and Thought* (New York: New American Library, 1949), p. 188.
2. Albert Einstein, *Living Philosophies* (New York: Simon & Schuster, 1931), p. 6.

3. As published in *Reader's Digest* (March 1959) with the following identification: "Former Governor Thomas E. Dewey of New York likes to quote this prayer, sent to him by William E. Robinson, who, in turn, received it from its author, a Mother Superior who wishes to be anonymous."
4. John Voris, "Let Senior Citizens Serve Others!" *Christian Century,* 77 (March 2, 1960), pp. 251-52.
5. O. W. Holmes, "There Shone the Stars," from *The Mind and Faith of Justice Holmes,* ed. Max Lerner (New York: Little, Brown, 1943).

Chapter Seven

1. Helen Keller, "Three Days to See," *Atlantic Monthly,* 151 (January 1933), p. 42.
2. Bennet Cerf, *Laughter Incorporated* (Garden City, N.Y.: Garden City Books, 1950), p. 7.
3. Arnold Toynbee, *Civilization On Trial* (New York: Oxford University Press, 1948), pp. 246, 248, 249.
4. Erich Fromm, "The Creative Attitude," in *Creativity and Its Cultivation,* ed. Harold Anderson (New York: Harper & Row, 1959), pp. 53-54.
5. Nicholas Johnson, "Test Pattern for Living," *Saturday Review,* 54 (May 29, 1971), p. 15.
6. Edna St. Vincent Millay, "The Spring and the Fall," *The Harp Weaver and Other Poems* (New York: Harper & Brothers, 1923), p. 22.